Three Chapters on Courtly Love in Arthurian
France and Germany

From *Le Livre de Lancelot del Lac* (ca. 1280)
By courtesy of the Yale University Library.

# Three Chapters on Courtly Love in Arthurian France and Germany
Lancelot—Andreas Capellanus—Wolfram von Eschenbach's *Parzival*

HERMANN J. WEIGAND

UNC Studies in the Germanic Languages and Literatures
Number 17

Copyright © 1956

This work is licensed under a Creative Commons CC BY-NC-ND license. To view a copy of the license, visit http://creativecommons.org/licenses.

Suggested citation: Weigand, Hermann J. *Three Chapters on Courtly Love in Arthurian France and Germany: Lancelot—Andreas Capellanus—Wolfram von Eschenbach's Parzival*. Chapel Hill: University of North Carolina Press, 1956. DOI: https://doi.org/10.5149/9781469658629_Weigand

Library of Congress Cataloging-in-Publication Data
Names: Weigand, Hermann J.
Title: Three chapters on courtly love in Arthurian France and Germany : Lancelot — Andreas Capellanus — Wolfram von Eschenbach's Parzival / by Hermann J. Weigand.
Other titles: University of North Carolina Studies in the Germanic Languages and Literatures ; no. 17.
Description: Chapel Hill : University of North Carolina Press, [1956] Series: University of North Carolina Studies in the Germanic Languages and Literatures. | Includes bibliographical references.
Identifiers: LCCN 56058693 | ISBN 978-0-8078-8017-3 (pbk: alk. paper) | ISBN 978-1-4696-5862-9 (ebook)
Subjects: Lancelot (Legendary character) — Romances — History and criticism. | Andreas, Capellanus. | De amore. | Wolfram, von Eschenbach, active 12th century. Parzival. | Courtly love in literature. | Arthurian romances — History and criticism.
Classification: LCC PD25 .N6 NO. 17

**UNC** | COLLEGE OF ARTS AND SCIENCES
Germanic and Slavic Languages and Literatures

From 1949 to 2004, UNC Press and the UNC Department of Germanic & Slavic Languages and Literatures published the UNC Studies in the Germanic Languages and Literatures series. Monographs, anthologies, and critical editions in the series covered an array of topics including medieval and modern literature, theater, linguistics, philology, onomastics, and the history of ideas. Through the generous support of the National Endowment for the Humanities and the Andrew W. Mellon Foundation, books in the series have been reissued in new paperback and open access digital editions. For a complete list of books visit www.uncpress.org.

# PREFACE

This study grew out of a lecture on the Lancelot theme delivered at the University of California, Berkeley, in April 1955. Addressing myself to a nontechnical audience, I was not concerned with the origins of that highly particularized cult of prowess and passion known as Courtly Love. On this much debated subject I would have nothing original to contribute. Neither was it my aim to present a historical or sociological study of the manners and customs actually prevailing at a given time in Western Europe. I was concerned rather with the creative imagination of an age that found its most brilliant expression in the verse novels of Chrétien de Troyes. Thus the emphasis of my title is on the *Arthurian* world, which neither poet nor audience equated with the world of reality.

But while writing this lecture I felt the need of expanding the scope of this study, first by adding a brief discussion of a famous Latin theoretical treatise on Courtly Love by a contemporary of Chrétien. Even more pressing was the urge to investigate the assimilation and modification of the conception of Courtly Love by the greatest medieval German poet, Wolfram von Eschenbach, in his *Parzival*. In this way something of a rounded picture of love under the dominance of the ideals of chivalry may be achieved for the half century extending from about 1160 to 1210 — this despite the fact that the lyric poetry of the troubadours, trouvères, and the minnesingers is not touched upon.

The long chapter on Wolfram's *Parzival* has a double justification. C. S. Lewis' admirable book, the *Allegory of Love*, makes medieval Latin, French, and early English poetry its exclusive concern. There is not even passing mention of Wolfram. The same is the case with Sidney Painter's *French Chivalry*. Specialized studies of Wolfram, on the other hand, though largely concerned with his French sources, tend to concentrate on other problems that arise in connection with his work. Having read the *Parzival* at least a dozen times in twice as many years, I hope that the discussion of the *Parzival* from the specific angle of Courtly Love will prove of special interest to the scholar without being too technical for the general reader. Needless to say, this chapter presented for me the real challenge. The focus of the inquiry involved a departure from the method pursued in the first chapter: here the procedure is systematic without any attempt even to indicate the outlines of the complicated plot. It is surely unnecessary to caution the reader not to expect anything like a balanced picture of the *Parzival* to emerge from a discussion that necessarily leaves out of account the Grail theme and the hero's religious development.

## CONTENTS

1. *Lancelot* .................................................... 1
   Chrétien de Troyes: *Cligès* ...................... 1
   Ulrich von Zatzikhoven: *Lanzelet* ............... 5
   Chrétien de Troyes: *Le Chevalier de la Charette* ... 7
   The Old French *Prose Lancelot* ................. 15

2. Andreas Capellanus: *De Amore* ....................... 18

3. Wolfram von Eschenbach: *Parzival* ................... 25

   Notes .................................................... 50

   Index .................................................... 57

# I

In his *Parzival* Wolfram von Eschenbach twice alludes, in almost identical language, to Lancelot's adventure of the swordbridge, and Lancelot's counterpart, the vicious knight Meleagant, plays a part in two episodes of Wolfram's vast poem. Facts like these may provide clues in the exciting adventure of lifting the veil that obscures Wolfram's background, his familiarity with French literature, and his way of composing. (For a scholar such a center of orientation as Wolfram behaves like a Geiger counter: it starts to tick when approching any area that is "warm"). But the story of Lancelot is an engrossing theme in its own right. In pursuing its fixation in literature we find ourselves involved with three quite distinct Old French works that have Lancelot as their hero. They tell such different stories that it would be more accurate to say that they have a knight by the name of Lancelot as their common denominator. The most archaic of them presents a Lancelot whose behavior shows no trace of the courtly lover.

If it can be taken for granted that the name of Lancelot, coupled with the theme of Courtly Love, evokes in every modern reader memories of a clandestine mutual passion between one of the greatest knights of the Round Table and King Arthur's wife, the subject demands the placing of this passion in a wider perspective, for the basic situation that governs the bond between Lancelot and Guenevere has much in common with that of Tristan and Yseut, wife of King Marc: there is the same consuming passion and the same resort to stratagem to obtain the consummation of an illicit love and to hush the voice of scandal. Both these stories, moreover, current at the same time, were for the first time cast in the polished literary mold of courtly verse by the most gifted French storyteller of the second half of the 12th century, Chrétien de Troyes. As if this were not enough, in the interval between his (lost) *Tristan* and his *Lancelot* Chrétien had composed another story that deals with the same theme — his romance of the Greek knight Cligès and the Byzantine queen Fénice.

Let me pass over the Tristan story as too well known to require elaboration in so limited a sketch as the present. As everyone knows, the love potion inadvertently drunk by Tristan and Yseut gives a peculiar, fated, irrevocable quality to the delirious ecstasy of this unhappy pair. The *Cligès*[1], however, equally famous in Chrétien's day, though now forgotten, is too remarkable a variant of the same theme to be passed over in silence. For one thing, it was conceived by Chrétien as a counterpart to *Tristan* (Wendelin Foerster calls it an Anti-Tristan)[2] in that it presents the love of the knight Cligès for Fénice, the wife of the Greek emperor, but uses a dodge to avoid a situation in which the lady would have to share her embraces between a husband and a lover. For another, it shows a very incongruous blending of an older plot that is farcical in origin with a treatment that lavishes some of the subtlest conceits, the most precious dialogue of passion, and the finest meditations on love upon this couple. And for a third, it not only climaxes their relations by the most shocking scandal but also contrives despite this to carry the story to a happy end. The story of Cligès, incidentally, like those of Tristan and Lancelot, is incorporated into the fairy-tale world of Arthur and his court. The story is briefly this:

Cligès, the son of Sir Gawain's sister and a Greek prince, is the rightful heir to the Greek throne. To assure his succession, Cligès' uncle, the emperor, has pledged himself not to marry. But when Cligès is fifteen, at the age, that is, when young Lancelot and Perceval also set out on their careers of prowess, the emperor, in violation of his pledge, makes arrangements to marry the incomparably beautiful Fénice, daughter of the German emperor. Cligès accompanies his uncle to Cologne for the wedding, and the moment he and Fénice set eyes upon each other, their hearts are exchanged though no word is spoken between them. Fénice, knowing her fate but resolved not to be a second Yseut, unburdens herself to her nurse Thessala,[3] who contrives at the wedding banquet to pass to the bridegroom a potion of rather complicated magic effect. By virtue of his drinking it he is barred forever from possessing Fénice. As soon as the couple have gone to bed he falls asleep and he dreams that he is enjoying all the delights of her corporeal embrace. This spell is permanent. It does not wear off in the course of years, and Fénice, though married, remains a virgin. On the journey homeward the Greeks are ambushed by the Duke of Saxony, who has prior claims to Fénice. In this situation Cligès saves the day by incomparable feats of prowess, and he rescues Fénice from a dozen Saxon abductors, killing eleven of them, leaving only one to tell the tale, like Tydeus, who comes off with similar glory in the *Roman de Thèbes*.[4] So the uncle not only has no rightful claims to Fénice on two counts, but Cligès has earned her. Even so, the lovers communicate only by glances. They speak not a word. After the safe return to Constantinople, Cligès, in obedience to his deceased father's bidding, sets out for Arthur's court. There he distinguishes himself by fighting incognito, in four different colored suits of armour, in a four-day tournament. On the first day he unhorses Segremors li desreés, on the second Lancelot du Lac, on the third it is the turn of Perceval li Galois to take a spill, and on the fourth he fights Gauvain (the standard paragon) to a draw. Then, recognized as Arthur's nephew and heaped with honors, he returns to the East. For a long time he and Fénice languish in each other's sight and practice superhuman restraint. But at last the secret of their mutual infatuation escapes their lips. Even now Fénice is as determined as ever not to indulge in a clandestine love like Yseut, which may set tongues wagging. She appeals to Saint Paul [!] as authority for her resolve at least to beware of scandal if total continence is too hard to endure. She will belong to him only, she says, if he will spirit her away to a retreat where she will never be recognized. Her plan is this: She will take a drug prepared by Thessala which will put her into a coma resembling death (like Shakespeare's Juliet). She will be entombed. In due time her lover will snatch and abduct her, and she will come to life in his arms. Since the kind of retreat desired is already at hand in the form of an ingeniously appointed tower, the plan is put into effect forthwith. It is on the point of succeeding when three physicians from Salerno, remembering a similar ruse played by King Solomon's wife, insist on trying to bring her back to life by blandishments, by beatings and tortures. They pour molten lead through her palms and even that having no effect, prepare to roast her. At this point the palace women, who have been secretly watching, can no longer restrain their indignation: they break open the door and hurl the fiends through a window to their death. Now Fénice is entombed with solemn rites and on the third night Cligès succeeds in carrying her off undiscovered. The handy Thessala's arts are again invoked to heal Fénice's cruel wounds and restore her to complete health and beauty within a fortnight. Now the two lovers enjoy fifteen months of unbroken bliss in each other's company. But in the long run the monotony of the tower begins to pall, and they install their bed under the canopy of a lovely tree in the adjoining garden, screened by a high wall. Then it happens one day that a huntsman, in pursuit of his strayed falcon, climbs the wall, comes upon the lovers clasped in nude embrace, and recognizes the queen. Cligès, sword in hand, gives chase to the startled intruder, who is doubly sure of the queen's identity as a result of her outcries. The huntsman loses a leg in climbing back over the wall, but the emperor learns what he has seen. By the time the emperor breaks into the tower, the lovers have fled, leaving only their trusted servant Jehan to bear the brunt of the emperor's wrath. The servant makes a clean breast of the matter and also tells the emperor how he has been duped all these years into believing himself to be the possessor of Fénice's charms. What is most astonishing is that the emperor himself is convinced by this story. Meanwhile the lovers have fled to King Arthur and told him their story. He assembles a great host to succor his nephew. But the warlike expedition proves to be unnecessary. The emperor, consumed by rage and shame, has died and Cligès and Fénice come into rightful possession of the throne and live happily ever after.

Obviously this fantastic plot is quite out of keeping with the hyper-refined sentiments of courtly romance. The machinery of the magic employed is much too complicated and too frequently invoked to allow credence even on a make-believe basis. The scandalous dénouement could not be more offensive, and as for the morality of the devices employed by the heroine to keep from sharing the embraces of both a husband and a lover, she would be laughed out of court. Yet we have here a couple who belong to each other by right, being predestined for each other by their signal beauty and having earned their mutual happiness by steadfastness and the observance of long and rigorous self-denial. *Cligès* is a curious blend of crudity and high idealism. In my retelling of it the former element has necessarily predominated, but the fact of the matter is that the ideal side was in the foreground of the poet's interest. He lavished thousands of lines on the artful development of the sweet passion, its symptoms, and their paradoxical expression in the reticence and pensiveness of the lovers. His ingenuity is inexhaustible in playing variations on the theme of the language of the eyes and the exchange of the lovers' hearts. He is full of allusion and imagery. His play with hyperbole reaches astronomical dimensions when he says: "If my wits doubled every day and I lived to be a thousand years, I could not begin to exhaust the praise of her charms;"[5] or when he says: "God, who fashioned Fénice, has not seen fit to bestow on any man a power of praise that could compare with the degree of beauty lodged within her."[6] This comparison of incomparables, yet somehow comparable in the mind of God, would afford a beautiful text for a whole discourse on the transcendental world as conceived by the medieval poet. But my reason for quoting these lines is their involved syntax. Here the central idea is shunted to a siding and the main track is cleared for an irrelevant circumstance. It is the sort of device not infrequently used by Wolfram von Eschenbach and most beautifully instanced in the pretty speech of the maiden queen who asks Parzival's help against her besieger, King Clamidé. "You see my crenellated walls and towers," she says. "Well, among them there is no tower so high that I would not liefer plunge from it to my death than accept King Clamidé's love." The sentence as uttered affords a choice of suicide from towers of varying height, and it is implied that the choice of the highest involves a particular degree of courage. Is there not a ripple of humor tinged with pathos about this confession uttered by the wide-eyed maiden?

\* \* \*

But it is high time that we turn to Lancelot. As I remarked at the out set, there are three separate stories to deal with in this connection. We begin wih the most archaic of these[7]—archaic insofar as it tells a story that caters to an audience that finds its entertainment in the narrative of a chain of adventures pure and simple. The spirit of Courtly Love as an essence pervading the chain of adventures is totally lacking. Whereas, since the middle of the 12th century, most traditional subjects from classical antiquity — the siege of Thebes, the Trojan war, the vicissitudes of Aeneas — had been completely transformed into vehicles of the sweet passion and gallant courtship, we find nothing of the sort here. An occasional touch reveals the author's acquaintance with the new emotional climate — that is all.[8] This story has been transmitted to us only in a German verse tale of some 9,500 lines. Its author, Ulrich von Zatzikhoven in Switzerland, names himself twice at the end. He tells us that he has put into German, adding nothing and omitting nothing, a French romance left in Germany by an Anglo-Norman knight, Huc de Morville, who was one of the hostages furnished by King Richard the Lionhearted in arranging for his ransom when he fell into the power of Duke Leopold of Austria upon his return from the third Crusade. From this we know that Ulrich composed his version after 1194. That is all we know. The French original has been lost, and there is no reason to think that it differed essentially from the German version. Unlike the great German masters, his contemporaries, Hartman von Aue and those antipodes of poetic genius, Wolfram von Eschenbach and Gotfrid von Strassburg, Ulrich was more of a pedestrian versifier than a poet. He had neither wealth of imagery nor ideas. At most we can give him credit for having given a charming turn to certain episodes.[9] His book, abounding in localities of magic character and in marvelous objects endowed with magic virtues, is a goldmine for the folklorist. We can be sure that the author of the French original trailed far behind his more advanced contemporaries in the art of poetic composition. It is impossible to give a halfway adequate summary of the events of Ulrich's rambling *Lanzelet* in the space allotted. I shall confine myself to a few essentials.

To begin with, Ulrich's *Lanzelet* is a biographical romance treating the life of the hero from his infancy to the end of his exploits. When his father's castle is stormed by his enemies the infant is snatched by a fairy who lives in a crystal palace in a magic lake. He is brought up by virgins who teach him music and by mermen who look after his physical development. When he is fifteen he is escorted to the abode of men. He is not told his name or his royal lineage, and he knows nothing of the arts of horsemanship or chivalry. But like Parzival and Gregorius he has a natural aptitude for learning these skills in a trice. In the course of many adventures he wins three women and marries them in turn. In each case he gets possession of the woman by fighting her nearest kinsman (father or uncle) to the death. The first of the three women is a mere windfall, a nymphomaniac, and he quickly leaves her. The second is sidetracked, never to return, when he falls into the snare of a magic castle that has the virtue of transforming all qualities into their opposite: having been the best of knights he languishes for a while in his captor's dungeon as the most craven of wretches. The third, fair Iblis, is predestined to be his permanent mate. She has a vision of him in a dream before he strikes the gong that summons her father, the redoubtable Iweret, to the combat which ends in his having his head cut off. Now a fairy emissary tells Lanzelet his name and lineage so that now he can present himself without shame to Arthur, at whose court he has already carried off the prize incognito in a three-day tournament.[10] It happens that at the very time when he approached Arthur's court, Queen Guenevere is in danger of being forever lost to the lord of the Round Table. King Valerin has asserted a prior claim to her hand, and the outcome is staked on a combat with the best of Arthur's knights. Sir Gawain[11] is already armed for the fight when Lanzelet arrives. But Lanzelet, having previously put Gawain under deep obligation[12] and also wearing a magic ring that makes his importunings impossible to resist, is given the chance to be the queen's defender. As is to be expected he defeats Valerin but he spares his life in a spirit of ill-advised generosity.[13] For Valerin, biding his opportunity, later abducts the queen by force to a redoubt from which she can be rescued only by the help of a magician. In this second rescue Lanzelet naturally plays a subordinate part. There is no hint in these exploits of any tender passion between Lanzelet and the queen. Now a fourth entanglement awaits him. Setting out in pursuance of an old quest repeatedly sidetracked (the avenging of an insult at the hand of a dwarf very early in the story) he performs an exploit that surpasses all his previous feats. In tilting against one hundred knights that ride forth to joust with him in turn he unhorses them all[14] and in consequence finds himself the lover of the queen, who has devised this test of prowess. Unfortunately she is possessive. Not wanting to lose her paragon-paramour she keeps him under close guard for over a year. He finally escapes by a ruse, swearing an oath that he keeps literally.[15] Now Lanzelet is reunited with his third wife, the beautiful Iblis. There is only one major adventure in store for him: a spell has been cast upon a maiden transforming her into a horrendous dragon. But speaking with a human voice the dragon pleads to be kissed, knowing that the kiss of the best knight in the world will restore her to human form. Lanzelet has the courage to oblige the monster and the spell is broken. This new woman causes no further complications and Iblis is secure in her husband's embraces. The story ends with Lanzelet's conquering his father's land and with his receiving the homage of Iblis' subjects. There are long drawn-out festivities in which Arthur participates, and Lanzelet and Iblis live happily ever after.

This story of Lanzelet has an agglutinative composition. It lacks any real structural organization. As for the hero, he is devoid of any distinctive character. If he is once called "der wîpsaelige" this is because it chances that all his adventures involve women and for the most part get him involved with women by fighting. It cannot be said of him that he fights in the service of the ladies. The conception of chivalry as an ideal is noticeably absent from this biographical romance.

* * *

We now turn to a second Lancelot story which has nothing in common with Ulrich's except the name of the hero and the fact of his championing of Queen Guenevere against an abductor. This is Chrétien de Troyes' verse romance of the Knight of the Cart, *Le Chevalier de la Charette*.[16] It was composed around 1170 and is some 7,000 lines in length. With this story we enter a realm of ideas and emotions of a quality so modern for courtly society as to be nothing short of sensational. In his introduction Chrétien tells us that he is fashioning this story at the bidding of his patroness, my lady of Champagne (*i.e.* Countess Marie, daughter of Queen Eleanor by her first husband, King Louis the Seventh of France). She supplied him with both the *matière* and the *sens* of the story, *i.e.* the plot and the idea or point of view. After having carried the story beyond its climax Chrétien left it to a brother versifier to finish (the last thousand lines), as we are told at the end. There has been much speculation as to the reasons behind Chrétien's abandonment of the story, raising many interesting questions regarding both substance and form, but we cannot enter into them here.[17]

In contrast to Ulrich, Chrétien's concern is with a single episode in Lancelot's life, the abduction of Queen Guenevere and her rescue by Lancelot, her secret lover. Chrétien plunges headlong into the story, mystifying his hearers, whetting their curiosity about the how and the why and even the who of the action, counting on the audience to piece together the background by scattered hints and leaving many strands hanging in the air.

The poem begins as follows: A vicious knight of superlative fighting qualities—we learn his name, Meleagant, much later—appears one day in King Arthur's hall and boasts that he holds many of Arthur's subjects, knights and ladies, prisoner in his land, the Land of No Return. Having finished his derisive speech he adds by way of studied afterthought that he is willing to stake their freedom on one condition: he will wait in the neighboring forest to see whether Queen Guenevere will make her appearance there in the escort of any single knight of the Round Table. He will give combat. If he loses he will return all the prisoners. If he wins he will carry off the queen as his prize. After his exit a hushed consternation grips the circle. It leaves us baffled, for only later do we learn, what they all know, that Meleagant is son of the King of the Land of No Return. And what knight, however brave, would gamble with the queen's safety on such a venture? Finally, by a ruse, the rash boon (a stock motif of current romance)[18] Sir Kaye tricks Arthur into entrusting the queen to him and he rides forth to the encounter. This leaves things at a desperate pass; for Kaye, though courageous, is known as a swaggerer, and all his exploits miscarry in a ludicrous way in whatever Arthurian romance we meet him. Heavy of heart, Arthur and Sir Gawain ride forth to see what the outcome has been, Gawain with a couple of spare horses to provide for an emergency. When they see Sir Kaye's riderless horse come in their direction, Gawain spurs on in pursuit. He is soon overtaken by an unknown (vizored) knight in full armor, furiously spurring his spent steed. Gawain obliges by giving him one of his fresh horses and he is soon out of sight. They meet up again later. This time the strange knight is mounted on a cart driven by a dwarf. Much later we learn (what Chrétien's audience may have guessed at once) that this is Sir Lancelot. Where had he been when Meleagant delivered his challenge? In a way never accounted for in the story he must have learned of the queen's predicament, flown to the rescue and come to grief. The breathless pace of the narrative leaves all these questions unanswered. His presence on the cart (or tumbril) calls for an explanation. In those days, Chrétien says, the cart was used only to transport condemned criminals. It was the mark of the greatest disgrace conceivable. Filth and stones were flung at one so conveyed. A knight who would venture to ride a cart, automatically became an outcast from courtly society. Why then had Lancelot mounted the cart? Because the dwarf had promised to guide him to the sight of the queen the next morning. In the symbolic act of mounting the cart we see Lancelot sacrificing all worldly honor for the sake of the queen to whom he is devoted with religious fervor. When Gawain catches up with him he is also invited to take a seat in the cart, which of course he declines.

We now follow the two greatest Arthurian heroes as they are bound on what seems an impossible quest, the rescue of the queen from the Land of No Return. They represent two types: the man of honor with the prestige of an envied reputation, and the unconditionally devoted lover. It is only the latter, we feel, who is destined to achieve the impossible.

The journey of the two toward the Land of No Return takes up a great deal of space in the story. Lancelot's quest is beset by all kinds of tests and trials that exhibit his willing submission to public shame (the ride through the castle gate), his unwavering self-esteem (though warned, he chooses the most splendidly appointed bed and is grazed by a lance with a flaming pennon), the intensity of his passion (having seen the queen led captive, he all but plunges to his death through the window), his single-minded chaste devotion (he cannot be tempted by his bedfellow, the lovely damsel, to touch her), his ecstatic adoration of everything regarding her body (he worships the golden hair left in her ivory comb), and, of course, his courage, his largess and his generosity (by various encounters). All this is shot through with the work of supernatural agencies, and a miraculous portent, his success in lifting the slab of a certain tomb, proclaims him as the predestined deliverer. We know now that his quest cannot miscarry.

There are just two ways by which to penetrate into the fastness of Gorre, the Land of No Return. The dark rushing water that bounds it is spanned by two bridges — a very narrow under-water bridge and a bridge, the length of two lances, consisting of the razor-sharp edge of a sword. When Gawain chooses the under-water bridge, Lancelot chooses the sword bridge and they pursue the separate courses indicated.

The crossing of the sword bridge tests another aspect of Lancelot's devotion to his mistress, his eagerness to submit to grueling pain on her behalf. He takes off his boots and his gauntlets; barehanded and barefooted he inches along the gleaming blade, perilously poised over the dark rushing water. He makes the passage, his knees, hands and feet bleeding from countless cuts. The physical torture leaves his wits unimpaired, for he recognizes the two roaring lions on the other side as just a mirage.

Lancelot's exploit has been observed from a tower by King Bademagu and his son Meleagant. The king, as highminded as his son is base, tries in vain to persuade his son to yield up the queen without a fight. Failing in this he goes to greet the unknown knight. He provides him with a physician, with a lodging, and with his best steed for the combat with Meleagant, which, despite his wounds, the knight refuses to delay beyond the morrow. As is to be expected, this combat is one of the high points of the story. Unperceived by Lancelot, the queen watches the contest from a tower. She alone knows the identity of her vizored defender. For a long time they fight equally matched but eventually Lancelot's strength shows signs of wavering because he has not recovered from his wounds. At this point one of the queen's ladies has drawn from her mistress' lips the whispered secret of her defender's identity. She raises her voice and calls out: "Lancelot, look!" He lifts his eyes and beholds the jewel of his devotion. The effect is stunning. He gazes at Guenevere entranced, heedless of the blows that Meleagant rains down upon him. At this critical pass the lady calls to him a second time. "Lancelot," she cries, "get Maleagant to stand between you and the queen." This inspiration turns the tide of the contest. Without taking his eyes off the queen, Lancelot leaps backward, and now the brute reels under Lancelot's irresistible blows. Try as he will, he cannot change his position. Meleagant yields step by step until they are so close to the tower that Lancelot cannot advance any further without losing sight of the queen. The king, fearing for his son's life, intercedes with the queen. She assents. The moment Lancelot hears from the queen's lips the word that spells grace for his opponent, he again stands immobilized, while the other exploits his unfair advantage until the king's barons forcibly drag him away. Even now the wretch will not concede his defeat. His face is saved by an agreement to yield up the queen provisionally but to contest her possession once more at Arthur's court after the lapse of a year.

Now the king, who has protected the queen during her captivity from his son's lustful advances, conducts Lancelot into the presence of the queen. But what is his consternation when she refuses to speak a word to her deliverer! Too fine a lover ("fin amant") to presume to inquire into the cause of her displeasure, he says: "Lady, indeed this grieves me; and I do not dare ask, why this" (3981-2). As she retires to an inner chamber his heart and his eyes follow her to the door. There his eyes well over with tears, and take leave of his heart, which follows the queen.

Having achieved his quest, including the liberation of all of Arthur's subjects, Lancelot's next concern is the fate of Gawain. But the next day on his way to the under-water bridge he is treacherously ambushed at Meleagant's bidding. He is led away, his feet tied under his horse.

The next phase of events is a flood of rumors, true and false, flying back and forth between the court and Lancelot's place of captivity. I neglected to mention that the whole region of the Land of No Return has an unexplained ultra-modern system of communications. Wherever Lancelot passed by on his way to the sword-bridge, his previous movements were already known, and we would not go wrong if we were to say that the queen had followed the whole course of Lancelot's adventures on a magic television screen. There is no explanation. Whereas the inner motivation of Chrétien's story is superb, flawless, the outward motivation of events as a cause and effect series is accounted for as little as it would be in a dream. The rumors we are concerned with now take on the configuration of poignant drama. The king hears the rumor that Lancelot has been murdered, and he vows vengeance. The same rumor reaches the queen and the shock nearly kills her. Her heart is filled with the sharpest remorse. "It is I who killed him," she laments. "Would that once ere he died I had clasped him in my arms. How? Forsooth, all nude to nude." (4243-6). She thinks of suicide but she feels she has no right to shorten her torments. For two days she takes neither food nor water, and her attendants believe her dead. Now the rumor of the queen's death reaches Lancelot. He is still in the position in which we last saw him, his feet ignominiously tied under his horse. He tries to make an end of his misery. Putting a noose around his neck, he commends the outcome to God[19] and slips out of his saddle, but his guards save his life. In his despair he speculates on what he may have done to incur his lady's hatred. Surely not the disgrace of riding in the cart, he muses. But as both the queen and Lancelot are wracked with anguish, rumors continue to fly ceaselessly. (We should probably say: rumor personified — the Vergilian *Fama*). The new reports tell Lancelot that the queen is alive and she in turn gets the news that he is only a prisoner. By an unexplained maneuver Lancelot is conducted back to court into the presence of the king, and now the king takes him to see the queen a second time. This second meeting of the lovers, unlike the first, is an exchange of tender looks and sweet words. At last our suspense and mystification, heightened by retardation and the participation in near-tragedy, are headed for relief. For Lancelot takes courage to ask the queen as to the cause of her anger after his combat. "How?" she says, "did you not feel shame and hesitation about the cart? You mounted very reluctantly and you held back for two steps" (4502-5). The realization of his sin strikes home. Love is an absolute, an unqualified imperative. "May God guard me against a second such misdeed," Lancelot says. "And may God grant me no mercy if you were not very right in your wrath" (4508-11).[20] All is forgiven and for the night the queen grants Lancelot a tryst before her window. At the appointed time he makes his approach with the proper stealth and they exchange sweet whispers through the heavy iron grill so as not to awaken the wounded Sir Kaye who shares the queen's chamber Lancelot longs for her embrace. If it is the queen's wish, he will come inside, he says. "Don't you see the grill," she replies, "so tough and strong that you cannot break or bend any of its bars?" "That is of no account," he says. "I do not think that any iron could hold me back if you gave me leave to enter. But without your full consent forthcoming the passage would be effectively barred for me." "You have my permission," she says. "But wait till I've returned to my bed, so that, should Sir Kaye awake from any sound, I'll not be compromised" (4615-44). This done, he bends the bars without a sound and without noticing that the cruel iron has cut his fingers to the bone. The lovers spend the night in blissful embrace and at dawn Lancelot steals away and bends the grill back into place.

There is a sequel reminiscent of the Tristan story. In the morning

## Le Chevalier de la Charette 13

Meleagant comes to the window and sees the queen's bed stained with blood. He accuses Sir Kaye of illicit relations with the queen. They both deny it; she thinks, in fact, she has had a nosebleed. In the wake of the clamor the king and Lancelot arrive. The queen's innocence is to be tested in a trial by combat and Meleagant is eager to accept Lancelot's offer that he substitute for Sir Kaye. Before the combat Lancelot swears a trick oath on holy relics vouching for the queen's innocence to the charge of her having slept with Sir Kaye. In this combat Meleagant is again worsted and a second time his life is spared at the queen's request.

The rest of the story entails one further trial of Lancelot's utter devotion to his love. Lancelot setting out to seek Sir Gawain a second time is again trapped by a ruse and imprisoned. Meanwhile Gawain, whose attempt to ford the under-water bridge has miscarried — he is fished out of the torrent half-drowned — presents himself to the queen. When a forged letter, purporting to come from Lancelot, announces that he has returned to Arthur's realm, Gawain has the honor of conducting the queen home. Only then do they realize that they have been hoaxed. The search for Lancelot yields no result.

Months later a great tournament is arranged by one of the ladies of the realm, and Queen Guenevere has consented to grace it by her presence. In his confinement Lancelot hears of the preparations. By pledging his word of honor to return, Lancelot prevails upon his keeper's wife to allow him secret leave to participate and she lends him her husband's steed and red arms for the purpose.[21] Despite his precautions he is recognized by a herald who, severely enjoined to keep the secret, cannot refrain from shouting when he sees him take to the field: "Here comes the knight who will beat the pants off everyone" (5583).[22] He keeps repeating this shout, calling much attention to the stranger. In the ensuing tournament Lancelot lives up to the herald's prediction without having to exert himself at all. As a result of this the queen is convinced he cannot be any other than Lancelot. To test him, she dispatches one of her maidens in attendance with a secret message bidding him to deport himself like a novice. Lancelot obeys, and for the rest of the day he has one misadventure after another and becomes the laughing-stock of the spectators. On the next day the queen sends him another secret message bidding him repeat his gauche performance and again he plays the rôle of the inept clown to perfection. The queen rejoices in the realization

> Que ce est cil cui ele est tote
> Et il toz suens sans nulle faille. (5894-5)[23]

that he and she are each other's, whole and absolute. Now she sends him a third message bidding him to do his best. As a perfect cavalier he replies that he is only too pleased to do whatever his lady bids him. He wears the same mien as when she bade him make a fool of himself. And now he sweeps everything before him. At the end of the day he eludes the crowd and sets out to return to his prison.

Herewith the demonstration of Lancelot as the perfect lover is complete. No further test of his absolute devotion could be devised. Nitze rightly observed that with the end of the tournament Chrétien's real task was finished. The rounding-out of the story could be left to an underling.

We know, of course, how the story must end, meaning by the story Meleagant's attempt to get possession of the queen—a single episode in the career of Lancelot; for we know that the story of Lancelot and Queen Guenevere cannot have the conventional ending of a happy marriage. Her place in the story was fixed as Arthur's queen, and her and Lancelot's clandestine love was a passion that was an end in itself and did not hope to eventuate in marriage. The end of the story can only be concerned with showing how the base Meleagant, that strong and courageous but otherwise wholly rotten hulk of treachery, finally gets his just deserts at Lancelot's hands. The vile wretch, thinking that he has left Lancelot to a death of slow starvation in an inaccessible tower, presents himself as agreed at Arthur's court with a renewal of his challenge. He feigns surprise at Lancelot's nonappearance and total ignorance as to his whereabouts. But Lancelot has been rescued. He appears in the nick of time. He exposes the whole shameful record of Meleagant's treachery, and having defeated him in a third, well-staged combat, he cuts off his head.

The story of the *Knight of the Cart* is the high-water mark of Courtly Love. This knight has not only all the virtues of gentle breeding — valor, generosity, largess, discretion, coupled with physical beauty and grace of speech and manners, he is not only willing to endure shame, humiliation, and torture on his lady's behalf, but beyond this he bears even his lady's displeasure without a murmur and honors her every caprice by unquestioning obedience. She on her part feeds the flame of the spirit that inspires him to do the impossible. In terms of modern sport this Lancelot shows a spirit not content with bettering the existing world's record in whatever he undertakes; his goal is rather to set an absolute record that will never again be equaled. Now all greatest ventures cannot hope to succeed without grace from above; so it is with Lancelot: an aiding and foreknowing Providence marks the chosen hero's path with signs and portents. It is not the Christian Providence, but an analogous power conceived as ruling supreme in a realm of its own — the realm of imagination and poetry.

\* \* \*

We must now take a very brief look at a third Lancelot story written in French prose by an unknown author not later than 1225, that is about half a century after Chrétien's verse romance. The first thing to note about this work is that it stands in sharp contrast to Chrétien's tale as regards both its scope and its spirit. Like Ulrich's *Lanzelet* it is a biographical romance, extending from the hero's birth to his death, and like Ulrich's it has Lancelot spend his childhood and adolescence under the tutelage of a water fay. But from the moment when the hero turns to knighthood his story ceases to have anything in common with Ulrich's. This Lancelot meets his fate as he first beholds the queen before he is knighted (she is then twice his age), and his whole career from first to last is governed by the flame of the passion that is then kindled. He is the exemplar of the High Fidelity lover. The *Prose Lancelot* is a compilation of enormous length. Let me say at once that Chrétien's story of *the Knight of the Cart* is worked into it as one of the episodes. But before you reach it you have to read your way through 684 large quarto pages in the modern printed edition[24] and the technique of progression is that of the inchworm. That chain of action that extends from Meleagant's challenge to where he has his head cut off amounts to a scant 70 pages (IV, 155-225), and it is followed by a well-nigh interminable series of other adventures. It is a safe estimate that Chrétien's story of the queen's rescue amounts to not one twenty-fifth of the whole work. What a profound sociological change since Chrétien's day must have occurred in the taste of the writer and reader (or audience) to lead to the assembling of a whole immense *corpus* of Arthurian lore! There is also a profound change of spirit. While Lancelot is still regarded as the most perfect knight of his time, in the *Prose* his illicit love for the queen casts a blemish on his otherwise spotless character, and a portent demonstrates him as unworthy because of this to succeed in the greatest quest of all—that of the Holy Grail. Time comes when Lancelot repents and vows complete continence, but the spell of the lovers' mutual passion proves stronger than good resolutions. Only after the death of Arthur and that of Guenevere does Lancelot find peace in a hermitage in a life of austere contemplation. When he dies, there are signs to indicate that he has won a seat in the gallery of saints in the heavenly choir.

The leisurely progress of the *Prose Lancelot* is accomplished by the repeated variation of all the stock motifs of Arthurian Romance. The compiler's limited imagination returned to the same themes again and again. The trials by combat are multiplied. The theme of the lifted tomb slab occurs at least three times. On three occasions Lancelot falls into a trance at the unexpected sight of the queen. Three times he goes mad for prolonged periods. He repeatedly spends long periods as a prisoner of some lady who wants him to become her lover. Four times he rescues the queen, twice he saves her from Arthur's fury for fancied or real transgressions. Early in the story the figure of his friend Galehot is invented as a foil for the base Meleagant, who is to make his appearance later. For, like Meleagant, Galehot also asserts a prior claim to Guenevere's hand, but unlike Meleagant he is the soul of chivalry. He already has the victory in his grasp when, in deference to the plea of Lancelot, whom he loves with a love amounting to worship, he yields himself a vassal to Arthur and renounces the dream of becoming lord over one hundred and fifty lands. It is Galehot's devotion that finds a way for Lancelot and the queen to avow their love to each other. To him there attaches no stigma of the go-between that has made the name of Pandarus, in the Troilus-Cressida story, a symbol of infamy. When Galehot thinks that Lancelot is dead he dies from grief—the most noble of friends.

To give a coherent brief sketch of the *Prose Lancelot* is, I believe, beyond anyone's power (I have not even plowed through all of it). For reasons of space it is likewise impossible to give more than an intimation of how Chrétien's *Knight of the Cart* has been fitted into its plan and with what modifications. As we should expect, the whole outward motivation, left hanging in the air by Chrétien, has been securely nailed down. We are told how it happened that so many of Arthur's subjects were forced to migrate to the Land of No Return; we learn about its geography and its extremely up-to-date system of communications. In the same way we learn where Lancelot had been held captive, how he obtained his release, and how he arrived in the nick of time as Guenevere was about to be abducted by Meleagant. We hear all about what happened to him before he came to the cart, plodding along in his armor on foot: he had displayed superhuman courage against one hundred knights lying in ambush but it had not availed him against Meleagant's dastardly and repeated treachery. More important than these matters, of which many more instances could be mentioned, are some important changes in the story. The most thrilling element of hyperbole is taken out of the sword-bridge exploit by having Lancelot crawl along it well shod and gauntleted, instead of bare of hands and feet as in Chrétien's version. The account of Lancelot's first public combat with Meleagant is modified, much for the worse to my way of thinking: here in the *Prose* Lancelot knows all the time that the queen is watching; he has much the better of the contest until the queen unwimples herself, when the sight of her beauty unnerves him; things fare so badly that Sir Kaye has to call out Lancelot's name and appeal to his sense of shame before his strength returns and he overcomes his foe. How different it was with Chrétien, where Lancelot, fighting with his eyes on his queen, had the strength of ten! The greatest modification, however, concerns the motivation of the queen's displeasure with Lancelot after the combat. It is made realistic and plausible, and a reader with a good memory can even anticipate its cause. For previous to Guenevere's abduction the treacherous Fay Morgan, who was holding Lancelot captive at the time, had sent a message to Arthur's court alleging that Lancelot had confessed to illicit relations with the queen and supplying fraudulent proof of this claim by exhibiting a ring, the gift of Guenevere to Lancelot, which Fay Morgan had stolen from Lancelot, deceiving him by the substitution of another just like it. Guenevere had denied the charge and defended Lancelot as incapable of such disloyalty, but she had been tricked into believing that his discretion had not been proof against the fay's wiles. No wonder then that she continues to be angry with him despite the valor he has displayed in achieving her deliverance. The episode of Lancelot's ride in the cart is, of course, also reported in the *Prose* (for the author of the *Prose* adds and duplicates but leaves nothing out), but no word is said about his having hesitated for the time of two steps before submittting to his humiliation, and this hesitation is accordingly omitted as accounting for the queen's anger. Thus this scene loses its superfine edge of absolute idealism. To judge by the immense popularity of the *Prose Lancelot* the realistic motivation accorded more with the courtly public's taste in the 13th century.

This completes our account of Lancelot. There are two topics left for us to discuss: the theory of Courtly Love as developed in a famous 12th century Latin treatise, and the reflection and modification of Courtly Love as it appears in Wolfram von Eschenbach's *Parzival*.

## II

The Latin treatise,[1] composed at the end of the 12th century, is the work of Andreas, a cleric, who refers to himself as the French royal chaplain. Inner evidence shows that he set himself the task of systematizing the conception of Courtly Love championed by Countess Marie of Champagne and her mother, Queen Eleanor. The treatise —some 200 pages in length—takes the form of a letter to his friend Walter, at whose importunings Andreas, putting on a show of reluctance, proceeds to instruct him in all matters concerning love. He goes about his task systematically, beginning with a definition of love and following it up with some further preliminaries. Andreas clearly has a three-part scheme in mind: 1) How to acquire love. 2) How to retain love. 3) Why love should be rejected. But the book did not work out fully according to plan. It spends most of its creative impulse on the first topic, how to acquire love. On the second, how to retain love, Andreas has very little to say. He soon runs out of material and turns to other highly interesting matters which would have called for a major caption, had he not been under the compulsion of a set scheme. This second division really deals with the casuistry of love. It presents 18 specific cases of issues arising in lovers' relations. Here the judgment of experts on the rules of love is invoked— great ladies, such as Marie of Champagne and her mother. And it concludes with a story in which a knight of Britain, after many adventures concerning the quest of a sparrowhawk, obtains a parchment on which the laws of love are written—31 in number—as divulged by the mouth of the God of love in person for the guidance of all true lovers. The third division, why love should be rejected, represents a total, most surprising about-face on the chaplain's part: contradicting everything that has been said in the first five-sixths of his treatise about the excellence of love, he assembles all the arguments that have ever been urged against the cultivation of the passion — religious, social, utilitarian, hygienic. And he ends up with a diatribe on women which ascribes to them—to all of them, without exception—all the vices recorded in his catalog. This satire on women (already a theme of classical antiquity) is an early instance of a genre that was to become a very popular vehicle of literary expression in the later Middle Ages and the Renaissance.[2] As regards Andreas, the very inferior quality of his satire would seem to show that he felt under obligation to pay some kind of lip service to the Christian code which as a cleric he was in duty bound to represent. His real interest lay in the exposition of the gallant passion in all its aspects. But as to his convictions, his set of values, the net effect of his book is to show an author who wears a mask, and we look in vain for a face behind it.

Disregarding the third part, we have in Andreas' book a manual of courtship and an exposition of the rules that govern the courtly lover's behavior. Love is extolled as the most ennobling of passions and the most exciting and hazardous of sports. The pursuit of love is an arduous service, a military service in a company of which the God of Love, *Amor,* is acknowledged supreme ruler. The whole conception of love is patterned on the Christian model, as its para-religious counterpart. For the realm of love has not only its God, but also its heaven, its purgatory and its hell in the afterworld. Their existence is vouched for by a detailed vision in which the constant are shown as dwelling in all manner of delight, the promiscuous as plagued by extremes of temperature and the mad press of confusion, and those who refused to enlist in the service of love as subject to cruelest torture in the life after death. (These unfortunates — beautiful women all of them — are seated on great rolls of thorns that are manipulated by savage attendants). Thus we see that the whole scheme is conceived in terms of the Christian set-up, as a parody of its scheme, but there is no overt humor to show it as a product of make-believe fancy.

The vision concerns the fate of women and is reported by a man. The whole book is written from the man's point of view and mentions the emotional experiences of women only incidentally — this quite in contrast to courtly romance, which delights in the infinite elaboration of the whole phenomenology of love, including all the symptoms of a nascent passion in both the sexes. Our author's chief concern is to instruct his reader, a man, in the ways of winning a woman on whom he has set his heart. There are three major, honest, ways by which a man can win the response of a virtuous woman — a fine physique, manly virtuous deportment, and fluency and elegance of speech. To the first and second of these our author pays homage, but it is the last which he sets out to teach. Given a bright young man, it should not be too difficult for him to learn the line of approach most likely to lead to the accomplishment of his desires. Medieval society being a class society, the approach must vary depending upon the social status of the solicitant and that of the lady. In both sexes three distinct classes are recognized as fit to concern themselves with the affairs of love: the middle class, the gentry, and the nobility. In the case of the male sex the cleric, because of his high office, ranks with the nobility.

Andreas casts his instructions in these matters in the form of a manual consisting of eight dialogues, in which men representing the three classes (and including the cleric) address themselves in each case to a woman of different social status. To exhaust all the possibilities of social degree there should have been nine, but the dialogue containing the line to be taken by a man of the gentry to a lady of the high nobility is omitted. These are schematic dialogues in which the conversation may take a different turn, depending on the age, physique, and affluence of the solicitant and the status of the lady as married, widowed, or virgin, and wealthy or indigent. In all cases, of course, the appeal of the lady resides in her beauty as well as in her virtue, and the man always represents himself as highly deserving of the requital of his passion on the ground of his virtue. Thus the dialogues, after the preliminary exchange of duly graded compliments, develop into a give and take of argument and persuasion. They are spirited rhetorical exercises that tax the aggressor's ingenuity, and they end with varying success for the male. For apart from the fact that women, too, develop a great deal of ingenuity in this sparring and do not always concede defeat in these debates, it would run counter to the courtly code for the male to win a complete and easy victory at the first assault. The fortress must be skillfully defended, and complete victory according to the code must be preceded by a long period of probation. There are four clearly marked stages in the attainment of a lady's favor: the granting of hope, the yielding of a kiss, the embrace or touch of each other's nude bodies, and complete possession. It is understood that the lady, after yielding the first three degrees of her favor, may always withdraw (for good reason) without conceding the most intimate enjoyment of her person.

Three things strike us as peculiar about the courtly code here unfolded: First, there is an axiomatic presupposition that love is a passion of supremely ennobling effect upon its devotee. The knight is propelled—impelled would be too weak a term—to all exhibitions of virtue by the glow infused by his lady. Feats of superhuman courage, acts of largess to solicitants, of generosity to the vanquished, are all owing to her inspiring grace. "Amor omnium fons et origo bonorum"—love is the fountainhead and source of all good things (68),[3] this is the axiom, ever repeated and developed by variation, throughout Andreas' book. Courtly romance, of course, is founded on the same principle. And who would deny that it has entirely lost its efficacy today, inasmuch as we are still poised on the brink of that *Brave New World* where a code of unadulterated promiscuous pleasure rules out all such sentiments except in that unfortunate throwback, the boy who still has an admixture of human blood in his veins, thanks to his Indian father, who thrills to Shakespeare's passions, who wants to earn his beloved by flagellation and torture and cannot adapt to the new dispensation of effortless enjoyment?

The second feature of the courtly code is the fixation of the lover upon one object. She has his heart in her keeping and the straying of his libido in other directions is, in theory, unthinkable. The embrace of the most beautiful woman other than his chosen is a thought that fills the true lover with aversion. There is no place for a Casanova in this society. A too active sexual constitution disqualifies from love.

The third feature is what sets it most apart from other sex conventions. "Marriage is no valid excuse for refraining from love" (184) — this is the first of the laws of love as formulated by the God of Love in person. A woman cannot appeal to her married status for refusing to entertain the solicitations of a lover. Marriage is viewed as a practical contract in which the relations of the two partners are governed not by love but by duty. The marriage relation lacks all the characteristics of true love, such as the blush, the pallor, the acceleration of the pulse, the delight of the furtive and clandestine embrace, the immoderate longing, the complete spontaneity, and that sweet frenzy of jealousy which escalates love to a higher and higher pitch. Jealousy in a married couple is as base as uxorious carryings-on between them are in bad taste (and even sinful). But the lover's *zelotypia* is an unceasing state of apprehension, a constant fear of not living up to his love's highest expectations, a perpetual delirium of trembling doubt, lest he lose her favor by his failure (103). We remember Lancelot's peril when, deviating by just a shade from the ideal, he allowed reason to debate with love for two steps' time before he mounted the cart, symbol of disgrace. This jealousy is the hottest flame in the innermost core of love's candle.

From what has been said it follows that a woman who enters into a contract of marriage has no right on this account to dismiss the man who has been her lover. It also follows that women who bestow favors on men with the ulterior object of inviting a proposal of marriage do not qualify as lovers. In all true love relationships secrecy is, of course, a prime condition as well as a stimulus of delight. A love that gets bruited about is almost certain to be shortlived. In any clandestine love a maximum of five persons may share the secret — the lovers themselves, two confidants entrusted with secret messages, and a discreet go-between.

The question of course arises how this precept of Courtly Love can be brought into line with the precepts of religion. The woman has scruples which the man glibly endeavors to dispel. He concedes that extra-marital relations are a sin according to the strict letter of the law, but it is an exaggeration to think that the deity is gravely offended by such a trifling transgression. Turning the religious argument upon her, he reminds the lady that the whole secular conduct of life is a continuous offense to God. If she is really concerned about pleasing God she should not be content with halfway measures but renounce the life of the world entirely. His advice is a paraphrase of Hamlet's "Get thee to a nunnery." To calm her apprehensions on this score, moreover, he tells her that there are two kinds of love, pure and mixed. Pure love is a graded series of solaces that may go so far as the nude touch of each other but stops short of sexual intercourse. This is unquestionably the nobler of the two, and he launches into a rhapsody praising its excellence and emphasizing that this is the kind of love he desires. At the end, however, he adds: "But I do not say this as though I meant to condemn mixed love, I merely wish to show which of the two is preferable. But mixed love, too, is real love, and it is praiseworthy, and we say that it is the source of all good things, although from it grave dangers threaten, too" (122-3). The real drift of this argument reveals itself in a later chapter where a question bearing on this issue arises: If a pair of lovers have pledged themselves to the observance of pure love only, what if one of the lovers then feels a strong yearning to pass on to mixed love? The answer is that the woman should yield: "But even if the lovers have made an agreement that neither may ask for anything more unless both are agreed to it, still it is not right for a woman to refuse to give in to her lover's desire on this point if she sees that he persists in it. For all lovers are bound, when practicing love's solaces, to be mutually obedient to each other's desires" (167).

It requires little sophistication to see how the manual of courtship here unmasks itself as a manual of seduction. This becomes most apparent when it is the cleric's turn to try to undermine the lady's defenses. To her untutored mind it appears a much graver sin for a cleric to indulge in the forbidden passion than for a layman. By no means, is his ready answer. God set down his law to keep for clergy and laity alike. It was not God's pleasure to create us as a special class exempted from the stings of carnal desire. So long as a cleric publicly conducts himself in keeping with his high office and with his tongue professes the true doctrine of the Church, such slight deviations from the strict command of the law can be easily condoned. He does not even blush to quote scripture in his defense of this position (125). And he gives a turn to the argument that presents him, the cleric, as the most desirable of lovers: Clerics are discreet by profession and wise. They are more sleek and well-fed than their lay competitors, and they are more readily available than the knights whose profession may require them to follow the summons to war at any moment!

At one point in the book Andreas gets personal and makes a confession. Speaking of the fact that a true lover can never desire the embrace of any woman but her who has his heart in her keeping, he says: "We know from our own experience that this rule is very true. We have fallen in love with a woman of the most admirable character, although we never have had, or hope to have, any fruit of this love. For we are compelled to pine away for love of a woman of such lofty station that we dare not say one word about it, nor dare we throw ourselves upon her mercy, and so at length we are forced to find our body shipwrecked. But although rashly and without foresight we have fallen into such great waves in this tempest, still we cannot think about a new love or look for any other way to free ourselves" (163-4). This confession, framed in the fictional content of the treatise, is wholly in keeping with its general scheme. It goes without saying that the man of experience advises his client with greater authority than the man who has only theoretical knowledge of the subject, and conversely, in the last part of his book, where he paints the love of women in the blackest colors, Andreas is at pains to emphasize that there is no way of getting so vivid a realization of the evils of love as by personal experience (192). We would therefore lapse into the autobiographical fallacy of a former generation of scholars if we were to rate the above passage as a true confession. As I said above, the writer Andreas is a mask and we look in vain for any face be

There is one more highly intriguing aspect of Andreas' book that must not be passed over in silence. We recall that the whole book is written as a personal communication from Andreas to his friend Walter. In one of its dialogues the speaker tells of an experience — a vision—in which he found himself face to face with the God of Love. The God in person recited to him the twelve major laws of love, adding: "There are also other lesser precepts of love which it would not profit you to hear, since you can find them in the book written to Walter" (82). Can there be anything more astonishing than such a reference? A character in the book refers to the book as something objectively existing! More specifically still: a fictional character (A) relates to a fictional character (B) that a fictional character (C) referred him to a later section of the very book in which these three fictional characters occur! We have the same thing in a later dialogue when the male speaker tries to prove the woman's conception of love wrong by appealing to the authoritative doctrine of Andreas, chaplain of the royal court (104). There is a third case of this kind when the Countess of Flanders, passing upon a lovers' dispute submitted to her judgment, cites the doctrine of the chaplain in support of her decision (172). These matters did not escape the attention of the learned editor of the modern Latin edition. He conjectured that these strange references might be later interpolations. But if they are interpolations, what other object could the interpolator possibly have had but to have some fun? For he was certainly not backing up the doctrine by any new authority! And if fun under the guise of gravity is the import and intent of these passages, why should they not be attributed to the author himself? He wrote every line of this book tongue in cheek. I think we have here some remarkable early instances of so-called romantic irony as practiced by Cervantes and Sterne, by Tieck, Brentano, and Heine, and, in our own day, by Thomas Mann.

It has often been pointed out that Andreas' book is in many respects a direct descendant of Ovid's *Ars Amatoria*, on the one hand, and, on the other, that it is deeply indebted to the Troubadour tradition of the Provence. Of the slant of the Troubadours Professor Nitze says: "A little ingenuity can trace all of these features [the illegitimate, the furtive aspect; love as an art, an accomplishment] to Ovid —provided we disregard for the moment the ideal that held them together."[5] While Andreas had a large share in the codifying of this ideal, we should hardly venture to call him an idealist. In this essay I have not touched upon the much debated matters of the origin, underlying social causes and development of the ideal of Courtly Love. By way of conclusion let me quote a statement on Andreas Capellanus' book by the late Professor Tatlock: "Few books have been so often referred to yet so little understood or even read."[6]

### III

In his *Dialogus Miraculorum*,[1] a compendium of recent miracles partly experienced first-hand, partly vouched for by creditable eye-witnesses, the devout Cistercian monk and good story teller, Caesarius of Heisterbach, discoursing on temptations—specifically the temptation to fall asleep during an edifying lecture—recalls an incident of his younger days: In the course of a homily delivered before the assembled chapter the abbot observed that quite a few of the brethren, including some who had undergone the stirring experience of conversion, were nodding and some even snoring. Interrupting his discourse he said: "Listen, brethren, listen. I have something new and great to tell you: There was a certain king whose name was Arthur." The effect of these words was electrifying. The abbot eyed his flock sadly, then said: "What a pity, brethren. When I spoke of God you nodded. The moment I inserted words of levity you came to and pricked up your ears, all of you eager not to miss a word" (Bk. IV, ch. 36).

This incident may have occurred some time in the first decade of the 13th century. At this time Arthur and his knights of the Round Table were the brightest constellation in the literary heaven of Europe. It was now more than sixty years since Geoffrey of Monmouth's fanciful Latin History of the Kings of Britain (1138) had recounted in great detail the warlike exploits of the matchless king in the British Isles, and on the continent against the French and the Romans. Some twenty years later the famous story was retold in French verse under the title *Brut* by the Anglo-Norman writer Wace (1155). Then, within the next three decades, the genius of Chrétien de Troyes created a whole series of French verse romances — an Erec, a Tristan, a Cligès, a Lancelot, an Yvain, and a Perceval-Grail romance, in which the emphasis shifted from warlike deeds to chivalrous adventure in the service of ladies and from Arthur himself to his knights of the Round Table. Each romance built up one particular knight as — for the time being — the matchless paragon of prowess, while King Arthur's rôle shifted from warrior king to ruler and representative incarnate of high-mindedness and courtly decorum. No longer primarily an active figure, Arthur became the gravitational center to which every knight of excellence was irresistibly attracted and around which the whole dynamic manifestation of courtly virtue revolved. Great as Chrétien's indebtedness to wandering minstrels must have been as regards names, motifs, and episodes, Arthurian romance, organized as a solar system with the king as central source of the light of chivalry, was Chrétien's creation.

This body of fanciful lore, fully developed by the 1180's but seized upon much earlier by a host of competitors, imitators, and facile versifiers, did not remain confined to France. German poets, both knights and clerics, took Chrétien's stories (along with French adaptations of the famous stories of classical antiquity) and rendered them into German verse, producing more or less free adaptations that preserved the outlines of the plot very closely, including much of its detail, but generally without that degree of adherence to the original which would label their work as translation in the modern sense. Thus the knight Hartman von Aue produced elegant, if somewhat sedate, German verse renditions of Chrétien's *Erec* and *Yvain*. The relation of Wolfram von Eschenbach's *Parzival* to Chrétien's unfinished Perceval-Grail romance, on the other hand, poses a unique problem. While Wolfram's account of Parzival and Gawan adheres to the structural pattern of its French counterpart and consists largely of the same episodes presented, moreover, in the same sequence, Wolfram's poem has an elaborate introduction (that gives the life history of Parzival's father and mother)[2] and it finds its way to a deeply satisfying conclusion. Beyond this, the spirit of the two narratives is utterly different. For over a century scholars in two hostile camps have searched on the one hand for a lost French version to account for Wolfram's deviation from Chrétien, and have tried on the other to vindicate the *Parzival* as the product of Wolfram's creative imagination. If, as I believe, internal evidence overwhelmingly favors the second conclusion, it is necessary to assume that Wolfram, in addition to being at home in the German literature of his time, had an extensive knowledge of contemporary French literature, including, more likely than not, all of Chrétien's romances,[3] the *Roman de Thèbes*, one or more other Arthurian romances that have been lost, and, of course, at least one work representing the Chansons de Geste, the *Bataille d'Aliscans*. The trouble is that it is hard to conceive how all these books should have been accessible to a poor German knight such as Wolfram makes himself out to be. It used to be regarded as axiomatic, moreover, that Middle High German poets confined their rôle to the transmission of foreign material and that they never consciously invented anything. The fact is that we are very much in the dark as regards all the major problems that crop up with respect to Wolfram's achievements. Whether he could read or write, whether he dictated his poems, whether he produced only one draft of his *Parzival* or whether it underwent repeated revisions, whether the first six books were made available to the public before completion of the whole, whether the spirited biography of Parzival's father Gahmuret marks the beginning of Wolfram's creative effort or whether this spacious portico to the great structure was added as an afterthought—all these matters have been much debated and have produced a wealth of incidental insight, but the answers have remained in the field of conjecture. The one thing, however, about which there can be no argument, is the high originality of Wolfram's personal style, his profusion of vivid imagery, his constant injection of personal asides, his ability to play with his language, to point-counterpoint the accents of his lines in studied contrast to the metrical beat of the verse, and to build up periodic sentences with multiple retardations and gyrations that unerringly reach their goal with a falcon's swoop.

All these matters lie outside the range of the present discussion. What concerns us here is the observation that the outstanding German versions of Arthurian romance, separated from Chrétien's originals by the span of at least one generation, tend to refine upon the courtly atmosphere of their model. For Chrétien, too, the Arthurian world is an ideal world of fiction, not only as regards the supernatural in the domains of magic and hyperbole; the deportment of his knights and ladies is an idealized version of the virtues and the accomplished manners and tone of conversation that prevailed in the high society of his day, but mingled with these elements there are still conspicuous remnants of crudity. A large proportion of Chrétien's combat scenes end with the victor's cutting off his opponent's head, just as heads off was the order of the day in the *Roman de Thèbes*, written about the middle of the 12th century. There is a grisly row of heads in *Erec*, and heads fly in Chrétien's *Lancelot* and in his *Perceval*. In Wolfram's *Parzival*, on the other hand, the crude primitive joy at the imagined sight of bloodletting is very much toned down. Wolfram's knights do not pull their punches, to be sure; we see the blood spurt in their fights, and many figures of secondary importance are reported as having lost their lives in tournaments. But here is the point I would make with all emphasis: except for the slaying of Ither by the javelin of young Parzival, who is as yet wholly rude and untutored, we are not presented with a single instance of Parzival's taking an opponent's life, and the same holds true for the second hero, Gawan, whose adventures account for one-half of the story. There is all the fighting spirit anyone may wish for, but no longer bloody battery for bloody battery's sake, such as the present-day movie audience is supposed to enjoy. There is, in fact, one combat of Parzival's (Bk. V) which would have had to end by his slaying his opponent, according to all the laws of chivalry. I refer to Orilus, who had slain Parzival's uncle Galoes and his kinsman, Schianatulander, and Orilus is the brother of Lehelin who seized the lands that belonged to Parzival by right of inheritance. Why does Parzival not kill Orilus, when a triple duty of vengeance would have obliged him to do so? The answer is, he does not know the identity of the opponent whom he defeats and whose life he spares on condition that he make amends to his lady of the tent, Jeschute, whom his jealousy had so cruelly wronged. A kindly Providence keeps Parzival — no other explanation is possible —from asking his defeated opponent to reveal his name.[4]

It is very evident that Wolfram does not want the stigma of a single gratuitous killing to attach to either of his two heroes, Parzival or Gawan. Let us look at the first of Gawan's adventures (Bk. VII) where there is fighting in deadly earnest and where Gawan is persuaded by the precocious courtesy of a little girl, who still plays with dolls, to fasten her sleeve to his shield and succor her father. In this fray Gawan encounters Meljahkanz (Meleagant), the notorious rapist, and we hear of Meljahkanz's being wounded and tumbled by Gawan and trampled under the hoofs of the victor's horse; yet the whole account compels the inference that Meljahkanz is rescued by his followers and escapes with his life.[5] And in the last of his series of adventures, on his way to Schastel Marveil, the enchanted castle, Gawan, having defeated a brave knight (Lischoys Gwelljus) who is too proud to sue for mercy, gives him a second chance, subdues him again, and takes him prisoner without exacting the pledge of his yielding his *sicherheit* (542,23 - 543,26).[6] Contrast this with a similar two-bout episode in Chrétien's *Lancelot*, where the worsted opponent's head flies off after the second engagement. Contrast this, if you will, with the stern justice of King Arthur in *Cligès*, where Arthur insists that the rebel knights taken prisoner by Alexander and put in the queen's charge, be surrendered to himself. Having them led into his presence bound, he passes sentence that they be drawn and quartered as an object lesson to the rebel host holding out in the fortress, and the grim execution is carried out, so to say, before our eyes. Thus we see that if we compare Chrétien's stories, written in the 1160's and 70's, with Wolfram's *Parzival*, written in the first decade of the 13th century, there has been a great tempering of bloody ferocity meanwhile; that is to say: leaving the conduct of actual life out of account, the ideal, fictional realm, of which Arthur is the center, is more consistently portrayed on the level of comparatively harmless make-believe. Knights are unhorsed and wounded aplenty (Keie in Bk. VI, Meljanz de Lis in Bk. VII, the nameless Grail knight whose captured horse leads Parzival to the hermit's abode in Bk. IX — to mention a few) but so far as the scenes enacted before us (in narration) are concerned, no one gets killed. Such killings as occur are either general and anonymous, as in the battles of Belrapeire, Bk. IV, and Bearosche, Bk. VII, and in the assault of the mob against Gawan at Schampfanzun, Bk. VIII, or they occur off scene (Schianatulander) or else they are reported long after their occurrence (Galoes; the heathen knight who wounded Amfortas with his poisoned spear, etc.).

The character of Wolfram's poem may permit the following formulation: It has come to be recognized at the time the Arthurian world reaches its acme of perfection that not only must the dénouement provide for a happy ending for the principal characters, but the spirit of play must be sustained on all levels of the action.

In Wolfram's *Parzival* the fictional Arthurian world is intimately blended with the theme of the Grail. However this theme may have originated, it appears in all the body of poetry devoted to its development as a legend revolving around the mysteries of the Christian sacrament of the eucharist. Thus it acutely poses the problem of reconciling the values of Courtly Love and chivalry with those of the Christian faith. The problem is very superficially skirted in Chrétien's unfinished *Perceval* (ca. 1180). It tends to an austere ascetic solution, setting up the ideal of absolute chastity, in the Grail story as imbedded in the old French *Prose Lancelot* (ca. 1225), where only the spotless Galahad achieves the quest. Wolfram's attempt to achieve a genuine synthesis of secular and spiritual values in the development of his hero, Parzival, sets him off from predecessors and contemporaries. We saw how glibly a cleric like Andreas contrived to blow both hot and cold. The deadly serious clash of the two sets of values as it presented itself to sincere believers can be illustrated by another story from Caesarius' treasure house of miracles.

Walter de Birbeck, Caesarius tells us in Bk. VII, ch. 38, was a young nobleman of great wealth and power, who distinguished himself in many tournaments. From his earliest youth he had tendered his particular devotion to the Virgin Mary. It happened that when a certain tournament was about to begin, Walter invited his companions first to join him in hearing mass. Eager to get on with the sport they demurred. He, however, entered the chapel and heard the mass of the Virgin sung for him. When it was over and he came out and inquired whether the jousting had begun, he learned to his amazement that it was finished and that he, Walter, had carried off the prize. How was this possible? Because of his great devotion to her the Virgin had assumed his shape, entered the lists, and won the victory.

In the same context Caesarius remarks — what may come as a surprise to many readers — that engaging in tourneys involves two mortal sins, the sin of pride (superbia) because it is done for worldly show, and the sin of disobedience because it is forbidden by the Church. Those who lose their lives in tournaments, he adds, are denied burial in consecrated ground. This was indeed the position of the Church. The earliest edict to this effect, according to Huizinga, was issued by the Lateran Synod of 1215.[7] We may ask how, under the circumstances, the Virgin could have felt prompted to engage in an activity calculated to set so bad an example, but it would be nothing short of impertinent to press this point and impugn her judgment. We learn, moreover, from the continuation of Walter's career that he was singled out for additional manifestations of a special grace. And do we not know on the authority of Dante, writing a hundred years later, that the Virgin on occasion has such power of compassion that the severe judgment up on high is broken? —

si che duro giudicio lassù frange (*Inf.* II, 96).

From Caesarius' account of this and other instances we gather that outward observance of the rules of piety counts for very much in obtaining the grace of heaven. The merest trifle of lip service or devotional gesture may spark the operation of divine grace and initiate the process of conversion. Yet despite his insistence on the observance of outward ritual Caesarius writes as a man of conviction and genuine piety. He has no patience with the kind of levity that condones a worldly life in youth on the chance of making amends by a devout old age. Nor does he mince his words in exposing the sins of the clergy. The practitioners of black magic in his stories are al-

*Parzival* 31

ways clerics — in this he confirms Chrétien and Wolfram, who report that King Arthur's wife was carried off to an enchanted castle by

un clers sages d'astrenemie (*Perceval,* line 7548)[8]
ein phaffe der wol zouber las (*Parzival,* 68, 4),

and it is in monasteries that the unspeakable practice of homosexuality abounds. The worldly life of German bishops draws his particular ire: they engage in warfare and bear arms like secular princes. "Is it conceivable," he quotes a Parisian cleric as asking, "that a German bishop should go to heaven?" (Bk. II, ch. 27)

For Caesarius the dualism of worldly and spiritual values is absolute. They dwell in separate compartments that do not overlap or even touch. But while theologians could be content with matters as they stood, freer spirits were straining to bridge the gap.[9] Conceding the separateness of the two spheres, they felt them as closely related by what Novalis six hundred years later called the magic wand of analogy — *der Zauberstab der Analogie* — each representing an ideal of virtue that has the power to fire the zeal of its devotees to limitless heights, to propel the emotions to infinite escalation. Wolfram was such a free spirit. He was aglow with a deeply emotional faith *and* he gloried in the display of the courtly virtues. His *Parzival* ends on the note of synthesis: to live in such wise as not to end up with pawning the soul to God's adversary *and* to enjoy the world's commendation nevertheless — that is the good life (827, 19-24; 782, 29-30). The same spirit of affirmation, the same desire to see life whole and to join what warring ideologies have riven asunder, accounts for Wolfram's tolerance and admiration of the Saracen world. Gahmuret on his first expedition to the Orient has a number of Saracen highborn youths in his retinue (18, 29). Heathen and Christian alike make up the captive population of the Magic Castle whose spell Gawan succeeds in breaking (659, 11-16; 699, 22-30). The childish, heathen, polytheistic idolatry that Wolfram attributes to the Mohammedans is their only flaw, but as regards all the virtues of chivalry, generosity, largess, and courtly gallantry, they are fully the match of their Christian counterparts. Neither creed nor color detracts from the nobility of their conduct. After describing the defeat of the black Prince Razalic, Wolfram pauses to utter the hope: "If he died without becoming a Christian, may God, for whom nothing is impossible, have his soul in his keeping" (43, 6-8).

The deep religious sentiment which pervades Wolfram's work is too complex a subject to receive more than incidental mention in these pages. Our concern is to see how Wolfram sets about modifying the ideal of Courtly Love and assimilating it to the Christian ideal.

Like all Arthurian romances, the *Parzival* is dominated by the mutually interacting interests of love and chivalry. The love is courtly in a literal sense insofar as all the principal characters are of royal lineage. The class consciousness of the poet and the society depicted bars the peasant from entering the precincts of Arthur's court (144, 9 ff). The base-born has only base, acquisitive instincts (142, 11 ff.). The townsmen also play a very subordinate rôle. They are devoid of the knight's sporting instinct. They fight only to kill when they take up arms in defense of their queen and have to be restrained from massacring the knights unhorsed (207, 17 ff.), and they riot as an undisciplined mob when called to arms against Gawan (408, 1 ff.). Love is the prerogative of knights and ladies. In their relations it is always present as an undercurrent. It intrudes even into spheres where we might not expect to find it. The lady who bears the Grail, and her twenty-four companions, are a bevy of beauties sumptuously dressed in the midst of a company of para-monastic knights pledged to chastity, and in the setting of the barefoot Good-Friday pilgrimage of the princely knight Kahenis and his family, the sex appeal of his daughters, dwelt upon at length, strikes an incongruous note (449, 26 ff.). The atmosphere of the *Parzival* is pervaded by the presence of *Frou Minne,* the German feminine counterpart of the Latin-French God of Love, Amor. She holds all-powerful sway over the emotions, for good or for ill (291, 1-30). Wolfram apostrophizes her in a passage that sounds like an echo of Andreas Capellanus' treatise. Evoking the memory of Heinrich von Veldeke, who in his *Eneit* (the story of Aeneas) was the first to treat of Courtly Love in German verse, Wolfram praises his predecessor: Heinrich displayed great art in working out the genealogical tree of Frou Minne's high lineage, but alas, he split the tree in two and gave us only one half. He told us only how to acquire love. Would that he had also told us how to maintain it (292, 18-23). This dichotomy of the subject matter of love, presented under the curious image of a tree branching in two directions, coincides with the announced plan of Andreas, but I am not prepared to say that such a division may not have been a commonplace of logical organization that both writers might have hit upon independently. We are on much surer ground when we state that Wolfram had nothing approaching a system in his treatment of love. The great variety of amorous relationships presented in the *Parzival* do not lend themselves to orderly grouping according to a scale of plus and minus values without injecting an element of arbitrariness into the scheme. It is easy to see, that is to say, where Wolfram's personal preferences lie, but he is careful to present relationships of alien character without suggesting any stigma of disapproval. It is difficult to generalize about his presentation of love. Two generalizations, however, can be made without hesitation: First, all deeds of chivalry, including Gahmuret's early exploits in the service of the Baruc, the Ruler of the Faithful, are engendered by love and admiration of women. Second, all love relationships aim at marriage as their consummation. Beyond this, we can be sure from the career of Wolfram's chosen hero, Parzival, that the single-minded unswerving devotion of a knight to one woman, who is his wife, elicits Wolfram's highest admiration.

As regards the first point, we may recall the French designation of the Crusades as *Gesta Dei per Francos*. By analogy, all deeds of chivalry related in the *Parzival* invite the formula: *Gesta dominarum per milites,* the exploits of ladies through the medium of knights. At one point in the story the great press of ladies in Arthur's cortège — each with her lover — is reported in just such terms: Here there are many proud young ladies whose bolts are nothing but jousts. They discharge their lovers against the enemy.

   manc werder man gein valsche laz,
   und manec juncvrouwe stolz,
   daz niht wan tjoste was ir bolz:
   ir vriunt si gein dem viende schôz (217, 12-15).

With this conception in mind we can understand why the scene of Orilus' jealous rage against Jeschute (when he believes her to have yielded her charms to the beautiul youth — Parzival — who left her in a state of disarray) is developed in very different terms from that of its prototype in Chrétien's *Perceval*. Chrétien gave a vivid naturalistic scene of questions shot at the lady as the ire of her outraged lord rose to the boiling point. By contrast, Wolfram's Orilus impresses the unwary reader as a vain braggart. He makes a long speech which begins by conceding that she, a king's daughter, lowered her rank in accepting him, a mere duke, as her husband. Then he proceeds to list all the heroes he has felled or killed — Erec, Galoes, Plihopliheri, ending with eight knights of the Round Table whom he downed — with herself and King Arthur as spectators — in order to vindicate her beauty as supreme in the contest for the sparrowhawk at Kanedic (133,6-134,5). But this is not meant primarily as a boast; even though his very name radiates haughty pride. It is rather a concrete way of recalling the heights of triumph her beauty had achieved through her knight, in order to show her how low she has fallen through her infidelity. A year later Parzival, long since knighted, defeats Orilus in improvised combat and compels him to be reconciled to Jeschute as the price of his life. This is the bitterest humiliation he can suffer, for he is still convinced of her guilt. "What does it matter", he says in effect. "I have lost all my honor through you, including this defeat. We're quits, so let us make up, since we must" (268, 14-18). His joy is correspondingly great when, after this enforced reconciliation, Parzival volunteers a solemn oath attesting Jeschute's innocence.[10] Another very striking illustration of the convention that represents the knight's deeds as in reality performed by his lady is found in the delightful episode where Gawan yields to the persuasive eloquence of a little girl, who still plays with dolls (372, 15-21), and agrees to fight as her knight on her father's side against two armies that besiege his castle. As he holds Obilot's tiny hand in both of his (371, 21 ff.) Gawan gravely tells her: "Let my sword be in your hands. If anyone seeks to tilt with me it is you who must ride this joust. You shall fight for me there. If I am seen there in the fight, this combat must be performed by you on my behalf" (370, 25-30). He wears her sleeve on his shield the next day and turns what was begun as a serious war into a tournament in which he outdoes all other contestants. When it is all over, Meljanz of Lis, who started the war and is now Gawan's captive, is told by Gawan: "It was no other than the hand of Obilot that took you prisoner" (394, 17-18), and Meljanz gives his hand in token of surrender to the little girl who is perched on Gawan's arm (395, 21-30).

Our second generalization, that all love relationships tend to find their consummation in marriage — this in sharpest contrast to Andreas' doctrine — can easily be verified by passing the principal characters in review. Gahmuret first marries the black queen Belacane and later Herzeloide. A third lady, Ampflise, to whose service Gahmuret had been dedicated since the time they both were children (94, 22 ff.) — she had knighted him (97, 25 ff.) and furnished him with treasure for his expeditions (12, 3-7; 94, 18 - 95, 4) — contests Herzeloide's claim and offers him her hand and her crown now that her husband, the king of France, is dead (76, 1 - 77, 18). Orilus and Jeschute are a married couple. Parzival marries Condwiramurs. King Clamidé had made war on Condwiramurs to compel her to yield her hand to him. Through Parzival's intercession he wins Cunneware de Lalant as a consolation prize (326, 15 - 327, 30). The war of King Meljanz of Lis against his fosterfather Lyppaut (Bk. VII) ends in their reconciliation followed by the wedding of Meljanz to Obie. The end of the Gawan adventure series is crowned by a fourfold wedding: Gawan himself has won Orgeluse; King Gramoflanz wins Gawan's sister Itonje; his other sister, Cundrie, is given to Lischois Gwelljus; and even Gawan's widowed mother, Sangive, begins a new matrimonial career as the wife of Prince Florant of Itolac (729, 27 - 730, 19). To complete the list of happy couples, Parzival's half brother Feirefiz embraces Christianity to become the husband of Repanse de Schoye, the virgin who carried the Grail. The general picture is not altered by the fact that there are a few irregularities. Feirefiz, the heathen, had had many loves, three of them mentioned by name (811, 8 ff.), before he won the Grail maiden, but the chief of these, Secundille, queen of India, had conveniently died before he took his new bride to his Eastern domain (823, 7). The Grail King Anfortas and his brother Trevrezent, forbidden the sport of chivalry in the service of *minne*, had violated the statutes of their order, bringing down upon themselves the wrath of heaven (472, 20 - 473, 3; 478, 1 - 479, 30; 495, 7 - 498, 6). As for Gawan, he is presented as the experienced man of the world, who has been in the thrall of the sweet passion many times (581, 30 - 582, 7) before he meets his fate in Orgeluse and ends up not merely as her lover but as openly acknowledged lord of her hand and her domain (730, 15-22). When he met Parzival, halted in a state of trance before three drops of blood in the snow, he knew from a personal experience which nearly cost him his life what a spell *minne* can weave (301, 8-20). And the account in Bk. VIII of his whirlwind courting of Antikonie, which was proceeding to full gratification when interrupted by an intruder (406, 28 - 407, 14), leaves no doubt as to the spontaneity and the sportsmanlike quality of his erotic responses (406, 1-15).

There is also the case of King Kaylet of Hoscurast in Spain, who jilted Alize, the sister of Hardiz, king of Gascone, after enjoying her embraces (67, 26 ff.; 89, 3 - 90, 6). What is more, he airs the subject with evident relish and he twits her brother about it, who has been tumbled by Gahmuret in the tournament and taken prisoner. Gahmuret effects a reconciliation between them (100, 21-2). Kaylet's conduct is certainly not in keeping with the rules of courtly discretion, yet the scene is presented without any note of censure. Kaylet, Gahmuret's kinsman, is a dashing young cavalier with an irrepressible tongue and irresistible charm (88, 7-19). He is "the life of the party" at Herzeloide's tournament. He is the opposite number of his very youthful cousin Killirjacac, who had already taken part as a lady's knight in the war against Belacane but was far too bashful to confess to such an errand. He parried the question put to him by Gahmuret with an exaggerated show of manliness (46, 7 - 47, 22). His secretiveness is not the discretion learned in a book of courtly rules. He simply marks a stage of the adolescent's development that his older companions have outgrown. The same motivation is apparent in the bashfulness of Parzival and Condwiramurs at their first meeting.

We would be hard put to it to find examples in *Parzival* of the discreet negotiation of a love affair prescribed by the courtly code. There are traces of it in the exchange of messages between Gahmuret and his royal mistress Ampflise, whom, for all we know, he has never seen since she knighted him, and in the first scene of the *Parzival* Gahmuret compliments his elder brother on his exploits as a furtive lover and expresses the hope of emulating him in this regard (8, 17-26). There is one extreme case of an artificially nurtured passion in a remote region of the story where the emotional climate is colored by the magic environment: King Gramoflanz loves Gawan's sister Itonje, who has been confined with her mother and sister in Clinschor's magic castle since her infancy. He has never seen her (607, 13), but the two have exchanged messages and pledges through an intermediary. They are madly in love with one another, and Gramoflanz sends Itonje a love letter that consists of a choice collection of courtly conceits. It is a classic of its kind and hailed as such by King Arthur himself (715, 1-30). This affair, further complicated by Gramoflanz' mortal hatred of Gawan, is also brought to a happy conclusion. Gawan's own erotic adventures are not of a nature to lend themselves to the application of the courtly code of furtiveness. Gawan is, of course, the perfect Arthurian knight by definition, as it were. Tact is second nature with him. He is recognized as "der tavelrunder hôhster prîs" (301, 7). But his secret messages to Queen Ginover and his precautions to maintain his incognito after he has won Orgeluse are not dictated by the courtly code of love. Their purpose is rather to stage a great triple surprise and bask in the emotional transports of King Arthur, his mother and sisters, and his mistress Orgeluse, as they simultaneously come to realize the full import of his marvelous exploits.[11]

If we except the hot-house flower of Gramoflanz' and Itonje's furtive passion, secretiveness appears in Wolfram's *Parzival* not as a courtly aspect of love but rather as a natural symptom of youthfulness. Wolfram took evident pleasure in refining upon the ideal of courtly society by dwelling upon the love of preadolescents and putting into their mouths the subtle conceits that were the fashionable tone of their elders. We saw such a relation in the childhood love of Gahmuret and Ampflise, which received only marginal treatment in the *Parzival*. An extreme instance of such a precocious passion is provided by the parallel case of King Arthur's son Ilinot, who fled his father's realm while still a child in order to dedicate himself to the *minne* and tutelage of Florie of Kanadic and who lost his life in her service. This childhood escapade is alluded to in but a single passage (585, 29 - 586, 11). Little Obilot, on the other hand, in importuning Gawan to take to the field as her knight, is presented in a series of scenes as handling the situation with the utmost decorum and gravity. She charmingly parrots the sentiments and the high-flown language taught her by her *meisterin*. Her discourse sounds like the reproduction of a text from a book of courtly manners (369, 1 - 370, 7; 371, 1-16; 23-30), and Gawan, perfect courtier that he is, enters into the spirit of the game and responds in the same tone. In Wolfram's second great poem, the *Willehalm*, the budding love of a pair of royal children is one idyllic feature within a setting of savage warfare: Alyze, the daughter of King Lois of Franze, and Rennewart, the son of the supreme ruler of countless heathen kingdoms, abducted and sold into slavery while still a infant, fall in love with one another. When Rennewart has grown into a young giant and is about to take to the field on the side of the Christian host preparing to meet his father in battle, the young lovers remember their pledge and have a secret tryst in which a kiss is exchanged (*W* 213, 9-28). The same background of youthful love is intimated in the *Parzival* regarding Sigune and her lover Schianatulander — in the first Sigune scene we see Sigune clasping her dead lover's body after he has been killed by Orilus, but the prehistory of this love is developed only in the unfinished *Titurel* poem, which is also ascribed to Wolfram, although, contrary to the *Parzival* and the *Willehalm*, Wolfram does not name himself as the author. The development of their preadolescent love forms the subject of the greater part of the first *Titurel* fragment. In a long series of strophes we first hear these two precocious children confess to each other the mysterious power of *Frou Minne* that forces them into indissoluble mutual bondage (*T* I, 47-73). As Gahmuret prepares to take his young nephew with him on his second expedition to the Orient, we witness the tender parting of the youthful lovers (*T* I, 76-77). Then, in the East, the adolescent boy's wan melancholy compels him to confide the burden of his passion to his uncle (*T* I, 88-107), while back home, in a parallel dialogue, Sigune unburdens herself to her aunt Herzeloide (*T* I 109-131). In these dialogues there are frequent references to Ampflise, who first nurtured the orphaned Schianatulander and used the boy as her go-between with Gahmuret to send him her missives of love, a fact that Herzeloide recalls with stirrings of suspicion and jealousy. All this embroidery is in keeping with the basic relationships sketched in the *Parzival,* and the intricate background of family kinship, there developed to a degree that staggers our comprehension, is constantly kept to the fore in the *Titurel.* The extreme elaboration of courtly sentiment and the wistful, melancholy tone of these dialogues may be accounted for by foreknowledge of the tragic end this childhood romance is destined to take. These *Titurel* fragments, whether Wolfram's own or the work of a near contemporary, were incorporated (embellished by internal rhyme) in the second half of the 13th century into a *Titurel* poem of more than six thousand strophes which was ascribed to Wolfram until modern critical examination destroyed this myth. This *Jüngerer Titurel,* as it is called, describes the scene of the final parting of the lovers before Schianatulander's fateful encounter with Orilus. He entreats the virgin Sigune to let him caress her nude breasts as a pledge of her love and she grants him this solace. A 19th century editor, Karl Bartsch, reconstituted these strophes and included them in his text of Wolfram's *Titurel,*[12] but later critical opinion has rejected them as spurious. There is nothing in this scene, however, which could be said to violate Wolfram's sense of propriety. His frankness in treating erotic situations leaves no doubt on this point. We do well also to recall the fact that Andreas' treatise included the mutual touch of the lovers' nude bodies among the solaces of what he defined as "pure love" in contrast to "mixed love," complete mutual possession.

The sad ending of Sigune's and Schianatulander's preadolescent dedication to *minne* and that of Ilinot should caution us against assuming that Wolfram's highly artificial and idealized world of Arthurian romance is all a matter of joy and festivity. "Who does not know that Joy is bounded by Sorrow?" Wolfram muses in a famous passage of the *Willehalm.* "Sorrow is the floor of Joy and the ceiling. Joy is walled by Sorrow on the sides, behind, and in front" (*W* 281, 11-13). The tragic undertone is never absent. For the most part it is

## Parzival

muted by virtue of the catastrophes being reported as having occurred instead of their being scenically witnessed. Sometimes it is very much in the foreground, notably in Herzeloide's foreboding dreams followed by the shocking announcement of Gahmuret's death from a heathen lance in the Orient. We are reminded constantly that death in a contest of arms is the typical fate of the knight who exults in his prowess and that the typical fate of the woman in whose service he fought is to die of a broken heart.[13] But the nobility of such an end envelops tragedy in an aura of glory. Ither's fate prompts the poet to pause in grief, but the point of this lament is not that Ither was killed but that he lost his life by a *gabylot*, an unknightly weapon (159, 5-12), hurled by a boy in fool's clothing. Again, the most typical situation leading to a tragic dénouement is that the lady in question is responsible for her knight's death: she held out on the reward so long that her knight was prompted to outdo himself in order to be worthy of her. She did so as a spur to further escalation of his prowess, and her grief and her self-reproaches on seeing what her idealism has led to are beyond bounds. The first case of this kind in the story is that of Isenhart, lover of the black queen Belacane. He responded to the test of his worthiness by giving away the most prized tent in the world — a gesture of unparalleled largess — and by engaging in combat without the protection of armor. When this display of bravado cost him his life, Belacane was inconsolable and reproached herself for having delayed his reward unduly (26, 10 - 28, 2). The second case, only parenthetically touched upon, is that of Gahmuret's brother Galoes, who lost his life in the service of Annore (91, 9 - 28). The third is that of Meljanz and Obie, which — contrary to the rule — is brought to a happy conclusion by Gawan's tactful intervention. Young Meljanz had solicited Obie's *minne*. She loved him dearly, but being filled with immoderate zeal to make the prize of her eventual possession a symbol of the highest attainment, she had couched her reply in the form of a farflung period that her lover took to be scorn (and commentators of the *Parzival*, who should have known better, likewise misinterpreted the tenor of her high-flown speech). This was her answer:

> If you were old enough to have devoted all your days for five years to fighting helmeted and under shield against extreme odds in such a way as to carry off the prize; if you then returned all dedicated to my service, and if I then yielded myself to your wooing, such a

favor would come too early. You are as dear to me (who can deny it) as Galoes was to Annore, who chose death for his sake when she had lost him in a joust (346, 2-18).

These are the sentiments of high-spirited adolescence. Young Meljanz, himself an adolescent, hearing only the rebuff and deaf to the concluding words of tenderness, went off in a huff and made war on Obie's father. The fourth case, dwelt upon at the greatest length, is that of Sigune. She reproaches herself most bitterly for the fact that she preserved the treasure of her virginity too long. Now that her lover has been killed, the remainder of her life becomes one unceasing gesture of devotion to his memory. She considers herself as posthumously wedded to him. She wears his ring. Insofar as thoughts can perform the works of love, she tells Parzival, she is his wife (439, 22 - 440, 19). Each of the four Sigune scenes is a variation on the theme of devotion. The first time, Parzival finds her holding in her lap the lover who had just been killed by Orilus (138, 9-23). The second time, more than a year later, we have the bizarre image of Sigune sitting in the crotch of a linden tree clasping her lover's embalmed body (249, 14-18). Years later Parzival finds her immured with her lover's sarcophagus in a newly built cell over a brook. Every Saturday Cundrie brings her her week's supply of food from the Grail castle. She is not a nun. Even though she has a psalter in her hand, her devotions are addressed to her lover. But this para-religious life is of the same quality and the same value as that of any Christian saint (435, 1 - 440, 19). Wolfram's account leaves no doubt on this point. The merit of this life is analogous to that of Herzeloide when she renounced her court and her lands for poverty and an abode in the wilderness. She did so in order to keep her son from any knowledge of chivalry, but this life earns her the heavenly reward (116, 15-21).

In all these cases, where the lady brings about her lover's death by an excess of zeal as regards his prowess, her rôle is that of the sorrowing repentant. That is wholly in order. But it would be an utter mistake to reason from this that she is culpable in the sight of the poet and that he uses her as an object lesson to others to guard against straining demands to the breaking point. On the contrary, the implication is that these women are to be admired for the glow of their zeal. Their fate evokes reverence and sympathy without the slightest suggestion of censure. I think the poet's sentiments would be rendered by the question: Could there have been such fine tragedies without such an excess of escalation? These ladies and their knights live and die in a climate of emotional hyperbole. The extravagant pitch of passion finds its classic formulation in the lament of King Clamidé after his hopes of winning the lovely Condwiramurs have been dashed by his defeat at Parzival's hand. As his seneschal, who suffered the same defeat a few days earlier, wrings his hands, his knuckles cracking like dry slats, on seeing his master rendering himself a prisoner at Arthur's court, Clamidé vents his grief in this magnificent outburst:

> Codwiramurs turns me gray. Pontius Pilate and poor Judas, who betrayed Jesus with his treacherous kiss — whatever torments their creator wreaked upon them I should not mind enduring; provided the Lady of Brobarz were my wife and I clasped her with her gracious consent, I should not reck what became of me afterwards (219, 23 - 220, 4).[14]

Such fire of courtly passion is one thing, sentiment is quite another.

As we now turn, at the last, to look at the love life of those characters who are manifestly closest to Wolfram's heart, we find an emotional climate of quite another sort prevailing. We find situations dwelt upon where natural feeling and spontaneity time and again break through courtly convention and reserve, where the irrational governance of passion and tender sentiment endows the characters with a generous human warmth that is absent from the exemplars of courtly conduct.

Parzival and Condwiramurs, despite their rôles of hero and heroine, scarcely afford the best illustration of this observation. Their first meeting is stiff and ceremonious. They are too young and inexperienced to be at their ease. Both are tongue-tied until Condwiramurs reflects: "It is up to me, I being the hostess, to speak the first word" (188, 25-30). And if it is love at first sight that makes Condwiramurs steal into Parzival's room that night and nestle into bed beside him, she does not know it: she has only come to implore the help of his strong arm against her besieger. The next day, to be sure, after he has defeated Kingrun, her natural feeling brooks no restraint as she proclaims: "This is the knight I shall belong to, or none" (199, 22-8), and that night they go to bed as man and wife, even though their union is not consummated until the third night (201, 19-23; 202, 21 - 203, 10). But except for a year of bliss, passed over very quickly in the telling, they live in separation for more than four years and a half, and though Parzival yearns for her as his one and only love, not even his longing for her can deflect him from his single-minded quest of the Grail. When they are reunited in the end, she having set out to meet him with the twins she has borne him, and he comes upon her asleep in her tent, she leaps out of bed in her chemise, wrapped in a blanket, to clasp him to her heart (800, 26 - 801, 4).

Love has a way of breaking through courtly reserve and affording touching scenes even in the case of some of the minor women characters. There was the lovers' quarrel between Meljanz and Obie in Bk. VII, where Obie vented her frustrated emotions in spiteful sarcasm, directed against her little sister Obilot and Gawan (365, 18-30). But when Gawan brings Meljanz into the presence of the court as little Obilot's prisoner and the little girl orders him to take her older sister as his *amie,* then Obie throws all courtly decorum to the winds: she stoops to kiss her wounded lover's bandaged arm and wet it with her tears (396, 25-30). Itonje likewise, despite her passion for Gramoflanz having been patterned on the model of utter secrecy, breaks down and weeps (710, 15) in full view of her lover's messengers (713, 1-10), who are certain to report to their lord what they have seen.

For the greatest examples, however, of lovers' behavior dictated by natural impulse and temperament in contrast to any conventional courtly code, we turn to Gahmuret and Belacane and Herzeloide. When Gahmuret, tossed ashore by a storm (16, 20-1), first offered his services to the black queen of Zazamanc, he did so in order to gain treasure (17, 11). But as soon as she has laid eyes on him she is madly in love with the young hero (23, 22-8). He kisses her (23, 29-30), offers her his services with a gallant flourish (24, 21-8), and before he knows it his sympathy for her plight has moved him also to love (28, 10-19). He spends a sleepless night tossing in amorous desire (35, 18 - 36, 4), and the next morning he unhorses and captures the chieftains of the besieging hosts, ending the war at one stroke. As soon as he comes into the queen's presence Belacane cannot contain her impatience to embrace him. She tells his pages: "Why do you cling to your master's heels, as though you feared you will lose him? You see to his horse. He will have his ease with me" (44, 12-16). And she takes him to bed straightway (44, 25-30). Wolfram lavishes all his art on representing Belacane as a paragon

## Parzival 43

of loveliness and sweetness, and Gahmuret loves her dearly. But the fact of the matter is that he has been trapped by the impulsiveness of his highly emotional nature. He is a lone alien in the realm of Zazamanc as to culture pattern, color, and religion. He has had misgivings from the first in laying eyes on all these black people (17, 26), and his sharp-tongued cousin Kaylet had put a barb into that compliment that felicitated him on his victories by saying: "If your subjects were baptized and of the same color as mine, no king could have a prouder army" (49, 13-17). It was Kaylet's observation presumably that made him give orders to stow away the priceless tent in his ship the next morning, when he distributed fiefs and treasure among his vassals (54, 12-16). The inevitable happens: after a few months of bliss as Belacane's consort he sails away in secret, leaving a message for the queen to find which told of his emotional dilemma. It complained of the fact that there were no tournament games among these people of alien culture; it contained profuse and genuine assurance of his abiding love; it held out the hope of his return provided Belacane would accept the Christian faith (55, 21 - 56, 21), but it gave no return address. And Belacane, after giving birth to Feirefiz, whose high royal and fay lineage Gahmuret's letter had detailed, died of a broken heart (750, 24-5).

A year later, at the tournament of Kanvoleiz, Gahmuret's impulsiveness gets him embroiled in a triple emotional dilemma. By being proclaimed the victor in the contest which the lovely virgin-widow Herzeloide had arranged in order to dispose of her person and her lands to the winner — again it is Kaylet's irrepressible tongue that brings the situation to a head (85, 5 - 86, 4); by having fought in the tournament as the knight of his childhood love, Queen Ampflise (78, 17-19), and by the fact of his being the husband of the black queen Belacane, whom he still dearly loves, Gahmuret's soft heart is torn in three directions. Gahmuret's susceptibility to woman's charms, like that of Gawan later, is accounted for by the poet on the ground of his fay ancestry —

sîn art von der feien
muose minnen oder minne gern (96, 20-1).

His emotional crisis is further aggravated by the news of the death of his brother, King Galoes of Anschouwe (80, 6 - 81, 4). Conflicting loyalties tug at his heartstrings. From the moment he first laid eyes on Herzeloide, when he rode into Kanvoleiz to the sound of fifes and drums, a gallant cavalier, one leg athwart his horse, the sudden twitch of his leg had told him that a new passion had taken possession of his heart (64, 4-8). Now, with the prize won but barred from its possession by conflicting triple obligations, Gahmuret breaks down and weeps. He protests that it is Belacane whom he loves and is bound to, and that only the denial of the sport of chivalrous tourneying made him leave her land (90, 9 - 91, 11). The depth of his despair is voiced by the charming defense in which he counters his cousin's reproof of his unmanly bearing (90, 15-16): It is certainly manly to feel shame when one wavers in his loyalty to his pledged love —

ez ist doch vil manlîch,
swer minnen wankes schamet sich (90, 27-8).

The situation is saved, of course, by the device of a courtly *minnegericht à* la Andreas Capellanus: Gahmuret promises to abide by the verdict and when it is rendered in favor of the lady in whose tournament he has participated, his joy knows no bounds: the showers of April have vanished and the sweet air of May has taken over (96, 12-19). To save his face, to be sure, Gahmuret stakes his consent to the verdict on Herzeloide's pledge to let him tourney to his heart's content (96, 25 - 97, 4). He further offers to continue as Ampflise's knight in his future tournaments though married to Herzeloide, but the French queen's messengers depart in anger without even deigning to consider his courtly solution (97, 25 - 98, 12). Here the formal pattern of the dénouement is that of the courtly French verdict, but who can fail to see that it is employed by Wolfram as a playful device to bring a heart-breaking emotional situation to a happy end? As soon as the matter is formally settled, Gahmuret and Herzeloide go to bed. Later in the day they emerge from their retreat and Gahmuret sets his highborn captives free (99, 29 - 100, 20).

Summing up the tragi-comedy of Gahmuret's predicament and the behavior that leads to his extrication, I would maintain that Middle High German literature has no other figure of comparable psychological complexity. There is not only a conflict of mutually incompatible *emotions*[15] (we have this at its most moving best also in the Ruedeger of the *Nibelungenlied*), but beyond this, Gahmuret's emotional conflict finds oblique expression. He cannot face up squarely to his situation. He rationalizes his conduct, putting forward acceptable reasons that serve to conceal the dominant drive of his personality from himself, if not from the reader. This Gahmuret, protesting, arguing, and weeping, says in effect: "I want Herzeloide more than anything else in the world, but I dare not admit this to myself." It is

Gahmuret who earns Wolfram the title of father of modern psychological humor.[16]

If Gahmuret behaves as a warm-hearted, highly emotional human being, for all his knightly trappings and the courtly discourse he knows how to use so well, the same is the case with Herzeloide, who is incomparably spontaneous in her emotional responses — a child of nature if ever there was one.

After Gahmuret's victories — he has captured four kings (85, 27-9) — she comes into his tent to greet him with the kiss customarily exchanged between royalty. Gahmuret's courtesy insists on his captives' sharing in this gracious salutation (83, 12-24).[17] He is both cagey and under a cloud of sorrow. They have scarcely sat down (on mats strewn with rushes) when she draws Gahmuret to her heart with an impulsive hug (84, 3-5) — a display of emotion toward a complete stranger scarcely in keeping with courtly decorum. The pretty speech she then addresses to him is also quite unconventional: She not only beseeches him sweetly to grant her his love, which she says is hers by right of his victory, but reversing the courtly situation, she sues for the grace of dedicating herself to his service (86, 29 - 87,6). Gahmuret is saved the embarrassment of a reply by Queen Ampflise's chaplain bounding up and asserting her claim upon Gahmuret (87, 7-24). Meanwhile Gahmuret's cousin Kaylet, who is also Herzeloide's uncle by marriage (84, 9-12), has sat down close to Herzeloide, and she employs her hands in sedulously caressing the bruises of his nose, cheeks, and chin (88, 13-19) — a transparent gesture that is certainly not lost on Gahmuret. The real matter at issue is tabled for the nonce, but the next morning, in the presence of all the distinguished contestants, including the "outs" as well as the "ins," Herzeloide formally puts forth her claim. When Gahmuret continues to put on a show of resistance to what he really desires with all his heart, she impatiently counters: "Let me no longer be consumed with longing"

Lât mich den lîp niht langer zern (95, 11)

and, brushing aside his further excuses, she insists on the matter being adjudicated, and thus she wins him.

The long honeymoon of the lovers now united in marriage provides the most colorful, uninhibited display of passion to be found in Wolfram's poem. Every time he rode forth to tourney, Gahmuret took a fine white silken chemise that Herzeloide had worn next to her skin and wrapped it around the armor that covered his neck. When he returned she would slip on the torn and battered garment to quicken the ecstasy of their embraces (101, 9-19). Eighteen tourneys were celebrated in this fashion. Then Gahmuret, summoned by the *barûc*, set forth on his second expedition to the pagan East and died a hero's death in battle.

Herzeloide's grief on hearing the dire news follows the same impulsive pattern as had been the case with her joy. When she recovers from her swoon — she is in her last month of pregnancy — she lovingly clasps her belly and her unborn child (110, 12-13). "God forbid that I should beat myself" [in a conventional show of grief], she says. "That would be Gahmuret's second death, since I bear the fruit of his love" (110, 14-22). Without regard for who might see, she bares her breasts; she caresses them and kisses their nipples, saying "You are the container of my child's nourishment" (110, 23 - 111, 2). In remembrance of her former joy she wants to put on her husband's bloodstained shirt that the messengers had brought from the East, but it is taken away and entombed with the lancehead that inflicted the mortal wound.

Two weeks after the catastrophic report Herzeloide gives birth to Parzival. He is so big a baby that she nearly died in labor (112, 5-8). With undisguised joy she beholds the manchild's genitals (112, 21-5). She nurses the baby herself, and in dwelling lovingly on the operation the poet shares in her maternal delight (113, 5-11). Herzeloide justifies this departure from courtly custom by thinking of the example set by the Virgin Mary, who deigned to perform the same office for our Savior (113, 17-21). A scholar of great learning interpreted this — her likening herself to the heavenly queen — as a symptom of madness.[18] To my mind nothing could be further from Wolfram's intention. In this as in her subsequent solicitude to keep the child from any knowledge of chivalry, she follows the natural instinct of a true mother. There is no trace of any courtly veneer attaching to her person in the moving scenes that precede her boy's departure from the forest to find the court of King Arthur. As he rides off without looking back, Herzeloide's heart breaks.

We have come to the end of our account of Courtly Love as reflected in Wolfram's *Parzival*. It is clear that the portrayal of Courtly Love as we found it in the romances of Chrétien de Troyes and in the treatise of Andreas Capellanus has undergone a profound transformation. If it appears that Chrétien and Andreas used the ideal fanciful Arthurian setting largely as a vehicle for portraying the courtly code and customs aimed at in the actual conduct of the courtly set of late 12th-century France,[19] the same is scarcely the case with Wolfram. To Wolfram and his audience the courtly French tradition must have appeared (and appealed) as something highly exotic and unreal. Wolfram's numerous asides make it quite clear that he was playing with an imaginary world that had little in common with life as lived in the upper circles of the Germany of his day. We could point to Wolfram's long speech in defense of Keie, for instance. In his telling of the story Wolfram presents Keie in his traditional rôle of pompous braggart, whose exploits always miscarry. Keie never appeared more vividly in a ludicrous light than when Wolfram shows him after he has come to grief as a result of his attack on Parzival — a bundle of pain and rage, venting his frustrated emotions in needling sarcasm directed against the perfect cavalier Gawan (298, 2 - 299, 12). But now Wolfram suspends the *story,* breaking the illusion of continuity by a forty-three line lecture to his contemporary German audience. "Let me tell you the truth about Keie," he says. "The story has maligned him. Keie was a man of severe integrity. That is why he was feared and hated by all the riff-raff that managed to crowd into Arthur's court. A stern disciplinarian of his kind, who beats courtesy into the ill-behaved when necessary, is just the person needed at the court of Landgraf Herman of Thuringia" (296, 13 - 297, 25). In the same way Wolfram turns the spotlight on contemporary reality when he says that he would not trust *his* wife to the press of knights and ladies at Arthur's court (216, 26 - 217, 6), or when he injects an incongruous note of realism into the account of the armies Gawan meets on his first adventure by mentioning the prostitutes in the train (341, 19-24). Wolfram's work is full of such warning signals that caution us against the fallacy of equating the fanciful ideal atmosphere of the story with conditions actually prevailing.

The system of Courtly Love as transmitted had no binding validity for Wolfram. Where Chrétien had done all that was possible in the way of setting a polished tone of parlance as regards the intercourse of knights and ladies, Wolfram went far beyond his French model in ennobling the manners and ethics of all worthy participants in encounters at arms. There is a spirit of gentle breeding and fair play, and intentional killings are, if not entirely avoided, at least reduced to the minimum required by the plot of the story. We saw that Wolfram does not develop either adulterous love or transient attachments; it is either the wish or the fate of all the many pairs of lovers to end in wedlock, unless tragedy intervenes. Thus love in Wolfram has more of the quality of passionate sentiment than of sport. Clandestine intrigue is not required to whet the appetite. In place of theoretical furtiveness, Wolfram develops the bashful secretiveness of adolescence and precocious childhood. His predilection for the latter, in a framework of extreme courtly decorum, greatly adds to the flavor of delicate fantasy in his work. If it is of the essence of courtly tradition that all deeds of chivalry stem from love, Wolfram points up this idea to its paradoxical extreme by picturing the ladies as performing the actual deeds of valor *via* the knights committed to their service, and when he thus has a little girl come off with the prize in the tournament he achieves one of his most delightful flights of fantasy.

If the concern of our inquiry had been Wolfram's actual ethics and his religious faith, we should have stressed the extreme value that Wolfram attaches to monogamous fidelity both in the words he puts into the mouth of the saintly hermit Trevrezent (468, 1-8) and in his own words of commendation (436, 1-22). His personal stand on this point being so clear, it is all the more remarkable that he manages to escort Gawan (whose antecedents follow a very different line) through all the mazes of his adventures without the slightest intimation of censure at any point. Wolfram finds severest words of condemnation for King Vergulaht's violation of the sacred laws of hospitality (410, 16-27), and King Gramoflanz' freakish sentiment in making a cult of his love for Itonje while lusting after the blood of her brother draws Wolfram's own disapproving comment (686, 28-30) and provokes his faithful go-between, Frou Bene, to the impulsive exclamation: "You dastardly dog! (ir ungetriuwer hunt! 693, 22). I think that the excessive use of retardation that gets the Gawan-Antikonie adventure off to such a slow start (Shall I, or shall I not tell you this story? 399, 1-10; 401, 24-30; 403, 10-11) shows that Wolfram was very ill at ease in treating this dubious episode in Gawan's career. But no stigma can attach to Gawan, whatever he does — this despite the fact that the contrast between Gawan and Parzival as regards the poet's degree of empathizing cannot be overlooked by any discerning reader. Gawan is the perfect knight-errant bent on worldly adventure;[20] Parzival burns with a quest to which he dedicates his whole soul. Gawan shares the limelight with Parzival and is a foil for Parzival in a story that forks, but Parzival is Wolfram's hero. Parzival, the man of inward zeal, is "the lord of this story." The strands of his heredity are exhibited in the great emotional romance of his parents. His birth is greeted with a shout of exultation (112, 9-12). And his re-emergence from obscurity, when the stage is set for the glorious finale, is hailed by Wolfram in one of the firmest lines of his poem:

>an den rehten stam diz maere ist komen (678, 30)

— this story has returned to its true stem.

No poet could be more emphatic than Wolfram in affirming the moral and religious values to which his spirit is dedicated. No other poet exhibits an equal degree of sympathy and tolerance for a set of values that have a different orientation. That is the paradox of Wolfram's *Parzival*.

# Notes

## I

1. Kristian von Troyes, *Cligés*, herausgegeben von Wendelin Foerster, Kleine Ausgabe,[2] Halle, 1901.
2. In his introduction to the text, pp. xxii ff.
3. The name indicates her rôle, Thessaly being known to classical tradition as the home of witchcraft.
4. *Roman de Thèbes* [ca. 1150], ed. by Léopold Constant, Paris, 1890, lines 1505-1784.
5.     Car se mil anz avoie a vivre,
   Et chascun jor doblast mes sans,
   Si perdroie je tot mon tans,
   Einçois que le voir an deîsse. (lines 2738-41)
6.     Onques Deus qui la façona
   Parole a home ne dona,
   Qui de biauté dire seüst
   Tant qu'an cesti plus n'an eüst. (lines 2721-4)
7. Ulrich von Zatzikhoven, *Lanzelet*, herausgegeben von K. A. Hahn, 1845. There is an English prose translation by Kenneth G. T. Webster, Columbia University Press, New York, 1951.
8. Lancelot and Gawan reprimanded for fighting without any knights and ladies to watch (2594-2622); Gilimar doing penance by a vow of muteness for an indiscretion committed against a lady (6572-6638); the spell cast upon Elidia of Thile for having transgressed against one of the precepts of love, and her being installed as arbiter in disputes about love after she has been released from her spell (7983-8040).
9. Notably the episode of the magic cloak that is tried on by more than two hundred ladies and is a perfect fit for only the most virtuous and most beautiful of them all (5806-6157). He also displays an astonishing color sense (4749-55).
10. He wore white, green, and red armor on three successive days.
11. Ulrich calls him Walwein, but to use this form of the name in my account would only confuse the nonphilological reader. Generally speaking, I have not aimed at pedantic consistency as regards the spelling of the Arthurian names in the works discussed.
12. By releasing his captive, Gawain's father, King Lot, without ransom at the end of the tournament.
13. W. A. Nitze and T. P. Cross in *Lancelot and Guenevere*, University of Chicago, 1930, p. 66, erroneously state: "In the MHG*Lanzelet* . . . he [Lancelot] is not even Guenevere's prime rescuer, this rôle being taken by Malduc." In a footnote Nitze credits what he calls the correction of Foerster's error to Jessie Weston.
14. He does not slay them, as Lucy A. Paton (*Sir Lancelot of the Lake*, London, 1929; p. 1) would have us believe.
15. Werner Richter, *Der Lanzelet des Ulrich von Zatzikhoven*, Frankfurt a. M., 1934, p. 3, fails to get the point of this trick oath. The circumstances are as follows: Four of Arthur's best knights set out to essay the adventure of

the hundred jousts in the hope of liberating Lanzelet from his amorous captivity. Arrived before the castle they give no hint of knowing him and he catches on to their intention. Karjet, as the first challenger, unhorses sixty-four of the queen's knights but fails on the sixty-fifth encounter. Erec, being next, tumbles seventy-three, but number seventy-four loses only his broken shield, not his seat. Tristan raises the score to eighty-nine, but in his next joust he runs his lance through his opponent right up to the hilt, holding him pinned in the saddle. Gawain finally disposes of ninety-nine, but in the final joust his lance carries off his opponent's helmet, leaving him intact. Now Lanzelet makes representations to the queen, insisting that his honor demands that he show himself in the field (6443 ff.). He swears a solemn oath that he will return to her as soon as he has had one tilt with one of the four (6482-90) and on this promise she lets him arm and mount. When the four see him charging in their direction they turn tail, pretending to flee, with Lanzelet after them in hot pursuit. The queen, realizing too late that this joust will be rendered on never-never day, falls in a swoon.

16. *Der Karrenritter (Lancelot)*, herausgegeben von Wendelin Foerster, Halle, 1899.
17. Did Chrétien protest against the ethical implications of the story he was ordered to write? Did he have a falling-out with his patroness? Did he feel that his version was a mere sketch, a first draft with many loose ends, and should be rewritten? Did he feel that the idea of the story had been fully developed at the point where he quit? Is this why he left the formal rounding-out of the episode for a pupil craftsman to finish?
18. Not limited to Arthurian romance. It also occurs in the *Roman de Thèbes*, in the Hypsipile episode, 2515-2646.
19. An outright attempt at suicide is thereby avoided, as in the case of the queen. Is this in deference to the Church's teaching that suicide is an unpardonable sin?
20. Lucy A. Paton, *op. cit.*, p. 36, quotes Lancelot as saying: "May God have mercy on me, if . . . ," thereby missing the full force of his penitence.
21. Cross and Nitze, *op. cit.*, p. 17, state that "she lends him the red armor and the horse of Meleaganz." This interpretation, though improbable, might be put on line 5519, but the context of lines 6079 ff. proves it wrong.
22. "Or est venuz qui aunera!" (literally: who will measure with the ell). Twice more repeated within the next ten lines and hailed by Chrétien as the first occurrence of a proverbialism.
23. Here the expression *toz suens* signifies love absolute. In *Cligès* the same words uttered in farewell made Fénice heave in joy and anxiety because they might convey no more than a conventional salutation (Cligès, 4385-4441).
24. *The Arthurian Romances*, ed. by H. Oskar Sommer. *Le Livre de Lancelot del Lac*, Vols. III-VI, The Carnegie Institution, Washington, 1910-13.

## II

1. Andreae Capellani regii Francorum, *De amore libri tres*, recensuit E. Trojel, Havniae, 1892; English translation with introduction and notes by John Jay Parry, *The Art of Courtly Love*, Columbia University Press, 1941.

2. A recent book by Francis Lee Utley, *The Crooked Rib*, Ohio State University, 1944, has brilliantly traced the history of this slant on women and its formal proliferation.
3. Page references are to Parry's translation, even when my wording slightly deviates from his.
4. E. Trojel, *Middelalderens Elskovshoffer*, Kopenhagen, 1888, p. 94.
5. Cross and Nitze, *op. cit.*, pp. 90-1.
6. In a review of J. J. Parry's translation, in *Speculum*, 1942, p. 308.

## III

1. Caesarius von Heisterbach, *Dialogus Miraculorum*, ed. by Joseph Strange, Köln, 1851; English translation by H. von E. Scott and C. C. Swinton Bland, London, Routledge, 1929. 2 vols.
2. Chrétien had employed this two-generation scheme in his *Cligès*. The first third is devoted to the story of the hero's parents. Cligès' birth is announced in line 2383.
3. Let me develop this briefly as regards Chrétien's *Chevalier de la Charette* (Lancelot). (1) Wolfram alludes twice, in almost identical language, to Lancelot's feat of crossing the sword bridge and his combat with Meljahkanz (Meleagant) shortly thereafter in order to deliver the queen from captivity (387, 1-5; 583, 8-11). (2) Meljahkanz is designated as a rapist already in Bk. III (126, 1-16), and again in Bk. VII (343, 23-30) but also as a very formidable fighter (344, 1-10). (3) Meljahkanz is the son of Poydiconjunz (344, 1), king of Gors, (348, 25) = Baudemaguz, king of Gorre. (4) Poydiconjunz has in his army a contingent of captive British knights, subjects of King Arthur. They are the most formidable part of his host (343, 22; 356, 17-20). (5) Meljahkanz, unhorsed by Gawan and trampled under the hoofs of the victor's horse, does not lose his life but is rescued by his allies (386, 30 - 387, 29). It is fair to assume from this fact that Wolfram knew that Meljahkanz was destined to lose his life in his final combat with Lancelot. (6) A very characteristic touch, the prototype of which occurs only in Chrétien's *Lancelot* (to my knowledge) is Gahmuret's posture as he parades with his retinue before Herzeloide and her ladies; he shows his nonchalance by riding with one of his legs athwart his horse (63, 13-14). This is the posture of one of the fiercest challengers whom Chrétien's Lancelot has to contend with on his way to the sword bridge. The knight's language is insulting but his posture is an exhibition of courtly nonchalance:

> . . . sor un destrier.
> De l'une janbe an son estrier
> Fu afichiez, et l'autre ot mise
> Par contenance et par cointise
> Sor le col del destrier crenu. (2585-90)

(7) On only one point does Wolfram deviate from Chrétien's *Lancelot* in his factual allusions: Meljanz of Lis rides the horse that his cousin Meljahkanz took as a prize from Keie (= Keu) in the joust which left Keie dangling in the branch of a tree (357, 18-26). This evidently refers to the queen's abduction, when Keu paraded as her champion against the

challenger from the Land of No Return. Chrétien omitted the scene of that combat, showing us only Keu's riderless horse galloping in the direction of Gauvain and the king, who have followed Keu and the queen in order to see the outcome. The *scene* of the combat is reported, but without Wolfram's characteristic touches, in the *Prose Lancelot*. Wolfram follows the version of the combat given in the *Iwein* of Hartman (lines 4669-82), who filled in the gap left by Chrétien (in the first of three brief allusions to the *Lancelot* in his *Yvain*) on the model of the biblical Absalom. In a later episode Wolfram has recourse to a similar picture when Parzival, in his joust with a Grail knight, is saved from plunging over a precipice by grasping a branch, as his horse goes over the edge and breaks its neck (444, 27 - 445, 7).

Seeing that Chrétien adroitly fitted the events of his *Lancelot* into the time scheme of his next work, the *Yvain*, by three brief allusions which recalled the abduction of the queen and her return with Gauvain to his readers (*Yvain*, 3706-15; 3912-39; 4740-45), it is tempting to try to fit Chrétien's story of *Lancelot* into the scheme of Wolfram's *Parzival*. This, however, proves to be impossible. Here Meljahkanz is a participant of that part of the Gawan story which occurs within forty days after Parzival had become a knight of the Round Table Gawan is on his way to Schampfanzun to vindicate his honor in combat with Kingrimursel, set for the fortieth day after Parzival's arrival at Arthur's court. That morning Parzival, entranced by the sight of three drops of blood, had unhorsed Keie, breaking his right arm and his left leg. Thus Keie could not have been in a condition to champion the queen against Meljahkanz for a considerable time. Moreover, inasmuch as Lancelot by defeating Meljahkanz after crossing the sword bridge had thereby effected the liberation of all the subjects of King Arthur held captive in the Land of No Return, this war, in which Gawan defeats and wounds Meljahkanz must have occurred *before* the queen's abduction and her liberation by Lancelot. If, on the other hand, we think of the abduction episode as perpetrated by Meljahkanz *after* his fight with Gawan as recounted in *Parzival*, Bk. VII, then Wolfram's allusions to Lancelot's exploit of crossing the sword bridge, defeating Meljahkanz, and liberating the queen, must be taken as an anticipation of a train of events still to come but uncorrelated with any of the events narrated in the *Parzival*. In the one instance when Wolfram permits himself an anticipatory allusion to future events of his own *Parzival*, he clearly designates it as such by using the word *sider* = *seither*, after these events: Gawan got his horse Gringuljete as a gift from Orilus, who got it from his brother Lehelin, who took it as a prize from a Grail knight whom he slew, a fact to which Trevrezent was to allude *sider*, at a later point of the story (339, 26 - 340, 6). Trevrezent does so (473, 22-30).

4. The remarks of R. S. Loomis in *Arthurian Tradition and Chrétien de Troyes*, Columbia University Press, 1949, on this scene (p. 395), as well as his numerous other attempts to use Wolfram's *Parzival* in support of his theories (pp. 350-1, 364, 398, 399, 406-7) are based on passages lifted out of context, distorted and misunderstood, and his errors are compounded by selfcontradictions. I cannot concede a trace of merit to Professor Loomis' arguments as regards Wolfram.

5. For a parallel incident see the account of the Battle of Salisbury Plain in the concluding section of the *Prose Lancelot, La Mort le Roi Artu*, ed. by Jean Frappier (Textes littéraires français,) 1954, p. 238, where Yvain, wounded early in the battle, finally is thrown from his horse. This is the sign for the enemy to charge the remnants of Arthur's host in pursuit. "Si passerent a cele empainte plus de cinc cens chevaliers par desus monseigneur Yvain . . . et ce fu la chose qui plus l'afebloia et qui plus li toli vigor et force." Despite this ordeal he manages to remount and fight again (p. 239). Cf. also *Parzival*, 38, 1.
6. References to Wolfram's *Parzival* use the double set of numbers — section and line — found in all modern editions of the Middle High German poem. The same system of numbering is used in the English Verse translation (with introduction, notes, and connecting summaries) by Edwin H. Zeydel and Bayard Quincy Morgan, Chapel Hill, 1951, thereby providing even the reader who is unfamiliar with medieval German with a handy and generally reliable means of checking the passages referred to. In my occasional references to Wolfram's *Willehalm* the double set of numbers is preceded by a *W*.
7. J. Huizinga, *Herbst des Mittelalters* (3d German ed., 1938), p. 111, n. 2. According to authorities cited by Sidney Painter, *French Chivalry* (Baltimore, Johns Hopkins Press, 1940), pp. 152, 155, tournaments were forbidden by the Church as early as 1130.
8. I quote the *Perceval (Li Contes del Graal)* according to Alfons Hilka's edition, Halle, Max Niemeyer, 1932.
9. The attempt to reconcile secular and religious values is very much in evidence in the work of the 12th century Latin poets of the Chartres School, Bernhardus Sylvestris and Alanus ab Insulis according to C. S. Lewis, *The Allegory of Love* (Oxford, Clarendon Press, 1936), pp. 104-5, 110-11.
10. The Lady of the Tent has a very rough time of it. Nevertheless even this episode serves to illustrate the difference between the place of woman in the *Iliad* and her place in the poetry of medieval chivalry. In the *Iliad* women are the prizes fought for and quarreled over. But Homer's heroes do not fight in order to display their prowess before women. In Bk. XIV Achilles, sulking over the surrender of Briseis to Agamemnon, works himself up into a mood of sentimentality: "Do the sons of Atreus think they are the only ones who love their bedfellows?" (340 ff.). But this does not prevent him, after the departure of the Greek embassy, from going to bed at the side of another fair captive (*ibid.*, 659 ff.).
11. Gawan's secretiveness is employed by Wolfram to the end of developing Bks. XIV and XV as a grand chain of surprises against a background of pageantry. Four great hosts consisting of knights and ladies in festive array meet on the plain of Joflanze in order to see the combat agreed upon between Gawan and Gramoflanz: (1) King Arthur and all his court. (2) The population of the Magic Castle freed by Gawan, including four hundred virgins and unnumbered knights. (3) All the chivalry of Orgeluse's dukedom of Logrois. (4) All the host of King Gramoflanz plus that of his kinsman King Brandelidelin. The surprises — not all of them joyful, but all destined to end in joy — include the following:

(1) King Arthur finds Gawan — whom he has not seen since the double

thunderclap of the two messengers of evil that branded the two greatest heroes, Parzival and Gawan, with the stigma of disgrace, four-and-a-half years ago (646, 1-8) — lord of the Magic Castle and lover of Orgeluse. (2) Arthur is reunited with his old mother Arnive, his daughter Sangive, and his two granddaughters, after a lapse of more than twenty years. The abduction preceded the tournament at Kanvoleiz in which Gahmuret won Herzeloide, who was to become Parzival's mother (65, 29 - 66, 8). Old Arnive's yearning for her kin had found moving expression before she knew of the surprise in store for her (659, 17 - 661, 2).
(3) Orgeluse learns that Gawan's secret message has brought Arthur and his host to witness the combat.
(4) Frou Bene, who had transmitted the messages and pledges of love between Gramoflanz and Itonje, experiences shock and indignation on learning that the liberator, who maintained his incognito, is the brother of Itonje and that very Gawan with whom Itonje's lover Gramoflanz proposes to fight a combat to the death (693, 21-30).
(5) Itonje is in a state of panic on learning that it is her brother who is to fight her lover. She is sure that her lover will be killed and that she will die of a broken heart (710, 9 - 711, 30).
(6) Gawan and Parzival, who have fought furiously without knowing each other's identity, feel the shock of mixed joy and grief when an end is put to their combat by the outcries of messengers who call Gawan by name.
(7) There is the joy and surprise of Parzival's rejoining Arthur and the Round Table.
(8) Gramoflanz, overcome by Parzival, is surprised to learn that it is not Gawan with whom he has fought.
(9) Parzival and Feirefiz, at the end of their combat, each recognizes the other as his brother.
(10) Orgeluse is taken aback in being presented by Gawan to Parzival and requested to kiss him whose love she had vainly solicited (696, 1-20).
(11) The second arrival of Cundrie, the Grail messenger, who begs Parzival's forgiveness and announces the joyful tidings of his election is, of course, the crowning surprise.

12. Wolfram von Eschenbach, *Parzival und Titurel*, 2nd edition, (Leipzig, 1877), III, 263-71.
13. Belacane (750, 25), Herzeloide (128, 18-22), Schoette (92, 23-30), and Annore (346, 15-18) all die of a broken heart.
14. The reader may be reminded of the famous passage in *Aucassin et Nicolette*, where the lover frankly states his preferences for joining lovely ladies and their male companions with all their finery in Hell rather than going to Paradise with the devout and wretched. But the hedonistic, flippant tone of the mid- or late 13th century *Cantefable* stems from a fantasy that is no longer keyed up by the tension of chivalry and Courtly Love.
15. In contradistinction to the rational casuistry of conflicting duties, which we find in Gawan, Bk. VII.
16. Gahmuret's self-deception is never explicitly stated, it is implied rather by the whole complex situation. The reader participates on two levels — empathizing with the hero and rising above his limited view of the situation.

17. Three of the four are designated as kings and their lands are named earlier. Only Lehelin appears without any title. Did Wolfram promote him to kingly status by anticipation in view of the fact that he was to turn up later, Bk. III, as conqueror of two of Parzival's hereditary kingdoms?
18. Samuel Singer, *Wolframs Stil und der Stoff des "Parzival"*, Wien, 1916, pp. 62-3.
19. Regarding this point the historian Sidney Painter shows an extreme degree of skepticism. See *French Chivalry*, pp. 140 ff.
20. Generally speaking, the question of reconciling his pursuit of adventure in the service of ladies with his faith in God and his observance of Church ritual never arises for Gawan. But there is one highly interesting passage where the two ways of life present themselves to him as alternatives requiring a clear-cut choice. This is in Bk. VII, where he is in a quandary trying to decide whether his pledge to meet Kingrimursel in the lists on the fortieth day will permit him meanwhile to incur the risk of being wounded (and defaulting on his pledge) in championing the cause of the little lady Obilot. His decision to incur this risk is motivated as follows: "Now Gawan remembered how Parzival had put his trust in ladies rather than in God" (370, 18-19). This is an echo of Parzival's words of farewell to Gawan when they parted company at Arthur's court. Parzival, feeling that God had played him false, counseled Gawan to put his trust in a lady rather than in God (332, 1-14). Nonetheless, before entering the tournament as Obilot's knight, Gawan attends early morning mass (378, 21-25), and the dilemma here posed is never alluded to again. Wolfram, fully aware of a basic difference in the motivation of his two heroes, obviously sidestepped the temptation of pointing up an antithesis.

# COURTLY LOVE IN ARTHURIAN FRANCE AND GERMANY
# INDEX

Absalom ...................... 53
Achilles ...................... 54
Aeneas ................... 5, 32
Agamemnon ................... 54
Alanus ab Insulis .............. 54
Alexander .................... 28
Aliscans, Bataille d' ........... 26
Alize (sister of King Hardiz) .. 35
Alyze (daughter of King Lois) . 37
Amfortas ................. 29, 35
Amor .................... 19, 32
Ampflise .. 34, 36, 37, 38, 43, 44, 45
Andreas Capellanus .. 18, 19, 20, 21, 23, 24, 25, 29, 32, 34, 38, 44, 46, 51
Annore .............. 39, 40, 55
Anschouwe ................... 43
Antikonie ................ 35, 48
Arnive ....................... 55
Arthur (Artu, Artus) .. 1, 2, 3, 4, 6, 8, 11, 13, 14, 16, 17, 25, 26, 28, 29, 31, 32, 33, 36, 37, 41, 46, 47, 50, 52, 54, 55
Atreus ....................... 54
Aucassin et Nicolette .......... 55
Bademagu (Baudemaguz, Poydiconjunz) ............ 10, 52
Bartsch, Karl ................. 38
Baruc, the ................ 33, 46
Bearosche .................... 29
Belacane ..... 34, 36, 39, 42, 43, 44, 55
Belrapeire .................... 29
Bene .................... 48, 55
Bernhardus Sylvestris ......... 54
Bland, C. C. Swinton ......... 52
Brandelidelin ................. 54
Brentano ..................... 24
Briseis ....................... 54
Brobarz ...................... 41
Brut ......................... 25
Caesarius of Heisterbach .. 25, 29, 30, 31, 52
Casanova .................... 21
Cervantes .................... 24

Chrétien de Troyes .. 1, 2, 4, 7, 8, 9, 11, 15, 16, 17, 25, 26, 27, 28, 29, 31, 33, 46, 47, 50, 51, 52, 53
Clamidé .............. 5, 34, 41
Cligès (Cligés) .. 1, 2, 3, 4, 25, 28, 50, 51, 52
Clinschor .................... 36
Condwiramurs ......... 34, 36, 41
Constant, Leopold ............ 50
Cross, T. P. .......... 50, 51, 52
Cundrie (Gawan's sister) ...... 35
Cundrie, the Grail messenger . 40, 55
Cunneware de Lalant ......... 35
Dante ....................... 30
Eleanor, Queen ........... 7, 18
Elidia of Thile ............... 50
Eneit ........................ 32
Erec ......... 25, 26, 27, 33, 51
Fama ........................ 12
Feirefiz .............. 35, 43, 55
Fénice ............ 1, 2, 3, 4, 51
Florant of Itolac .............. 35
Florie of Kanadic ............. 37
Foerster, Wendelin .... 2, 50, 51
Frappier, Jean ................ 54
Gahmuret .. 27, 31, 33, 34, 35, 36, 37, 39, 42, 43, 44, 45, 46, 52, 55
Galahad ..................... 29
Galehot ...................... 16
Galoes ...... 28, 29, 33, 39, 40, 43
Gawain (Gauvain, Gawan, Walwein) 2, 3, 6, 8, 9, 10, 11, 13, 26, 28, 29, 32, 34, 35, 36, 37, 42, 43, 47, 48, 50, 51, 53, 54, 55, 56
Geoffrey of Monmouth ........ 25
Gilimar ...................... 50
Gorre (Gors), Land of No Return 10, 52
Gotfrid von Strassburg ......... 5
Grail ...... 15, 32, 35, 40, 42, 53
Gramoflanz .. 35, 36, 42, 48, 54, 55
Gregorius ..................... 6
Gringuljete ................... 53

# Index

Guenevere (Guenievre, Ginover) 1, 6, 7, 8, 10, 13, 14, 16, 17, 36, 50
Hahn, K. A. .................. 50
Hardiz of Gascone ........... 35
Hartman von Aue ...... 5, 26, 53
Heine ....................... 24
Heinrich von Veldeke .......... 32
Herman, Landgraf of Thuringia .. 47
Herzeloide .. 34, 36, 38, 39, 40, 42, 43, 44, 45, 46, 52, 55
Hilka, Alfons ................. 54
Homer ....................... 54
Huc de Morville .............. 5
Huizinga, J. ............... 30, 54
Huxley, Aldous ............... 21
Hypsipile .................... 51
Iblis ...................... 6, 7
Iliad ........................ 54
Ilinot .................... 37, 38
Isenhart ..................... 39
Iseut (see Yseut)
Ither .................... 28, 39
Itonje ........ 35, 36, 42, 48, 55
Iwein (Yvain) ............... 53
Iweret ....................... 6
Jehan ........................ 4
Jeschute ............ 28, 33, 34
Jesus .................... 41, 46
Judas ....................... 41
Joflanze ..................... 54
Juliet ........................ 3
Kahenis ..................... 32
Kanedic ..................... 34
Kanvoleiz ................ 43, 55
Karjet ....................... 51
Kaye (Keu, Keie) ... 8, 12, 13, 29, 47, 52, 53
Kaylet of Hoscurast .. 35, 43, 45
Killirjacac ................... 36
Kingrimursel .............. 53, 56
Kingrun ..................... 41
Lancelot (Lanzelet) .. 1, 2, 3, 5, 6, 7, 8, 9, 10, 11, 12, 13, 14, 15, 16, 17, 18, 21, 25, 27, 28, 29, 50, 51, 52, 53
Land of No Return (see Gorre, Gors) 8, 9, 10, 11, 16, 53
Lehelin .............. 28, 53, 56
Leopold, Duke of Austria ....... 5

Lewis, C. S. ................. 54
Lischois Gwelljus ......... 28, 35
Logrois ..................... 54
Lois, King of France .......... 37
Loomis, R. S. ................ 53
Lot ......................... 50
Louis VII, King of France .... 8
Lyppaut .................... 35
Malduc ...................... 50
Mann, Thomas ................ 24
Marc ........................ 1
Marie of Champagne ........ 7, 18
Mary, the Virgin .......... 30, 46
Meleagant (Meljahkanz) .. 1, 8, 9, 10, 11, 13, 14, 15, 16, 17, 28, 51, 52, 53
Meljanz de Lis .. 29, 34, 35, 39, 40, 42, 52
Minne, Frou .............. 32, 37
Morgan, Bayard Quincy ........ 54
Morgan, the Fay ............. 17
Nibelungenlied ............... 44
Nitze, W. A. .. 14, 24, 50, 51, 52
Novalis ..................... 31
Obie ............ 35, 39, 40, 42
Obilot ............ 34, 37, 42, 56
Orgeluse ......... 35, 36, 54, 55
Orilus .. 28, 33, 34, 37, 38, 40, 53
Ovid ........................ 24
Painter, Sidney ............ 54, 56
Pandarus .................... 16
Parry, John Jay ........... 51, 52
Parzival (Perceval) .. 1, 2, 3, 5, 6, 18, 25, 26, 27, 28, 29, 31, 32, 33, 34, 35, 36, 37, 38, 39, 40, 41, 42, 46, 47, 48, 49, 53, 54, 55, 56
Paton, Lucy A. ............ 50, 51
Paul, Saint .................. 3
Pilate, Pontius .............. 41
Plihopliheri ................. 33
Poydiconjunz ................ 52
Razalic ..................... 31
Rennewart .................. 37
Repanse de Schoie ............ 35
Richard the Lionhearted ........ 5
Richter, Werner ............. 50
Ruedeger ................... 44
Sangive .................. 35, 55
Schampfanzun .......... 29, 53

Schastel Marveil .... 28, 31, 54, 55
Schianatulander .... 28, 29, 37, 38
Schoette ...................... 55
Scott, E. ..................... 52
Secundille ................... 35
Segremors ................... 3
Shakespeare ............... 3, 21
Sigune ............... 37, 38, 40
Singer, Samuel ............... 56
Solomon, King ................ 3
Sommer, H. Oskar ........... 51
Sterne ....................... 24
Strange, Joseph .............. 52
Tatlock, J. S. P. ............. 25
Thèbes, Roman de .. 2, 5, 26, 27, 50, 51
Thessala ................... 2, 3
Tieck ....................... 24
Titurel .............. 37, 38, 55
Titurel, der Jüngere .......... 38
Trevrezent ............ 35, 48, 53
Tristan .......... 1, 2, 12, 25, 51
Troilus - Cressida ............. 16
Trojel, E. ................ 51, 52

Troy, War of ................. 5
Tydeus ...................... 2
Ulrich von Zatzikhoven .. 5, 6, 7, 8, 15, 50
Utley, Francis Lee ........... 52
Valerin ...................... 6
Vergil ....................... 12
Vergulaht ................... 48
Wace ....................... 25
Walter (Andreas' friend) .. 18, 24
Walter de Birbeck ........... 30
Walwein (see Gawain) ....... 50
Webster, Kenneth G. T. ...... 50
Weston, Jessie .............. 50
Willehalm ............ 37, 38, 54
Wolfram von Eschenbach .. 1, 4, 5, 18, 26, 27, 28, 29, 31, 32, 33, 37, 38, 41, 42, 44, 45, 46, 47, 48, 49, 52, 53, 54, 55, 56
Yseut (Iseut, Isolde) ...... 1, 2, 3
Yvain (see Iwein) .. 25, 26, 53, 54
Zazamanc ................. 42, 43
Zeydel, Edwin H. ............ 54